CertPrimer 801

IBM® Lotus Notes® Domino®
Exam 801 Certification Primer

Randy Smith
IBM Certified Advanced Instructor
IBM Certified Advanced Professional for Lotus Software

CertPrimer™

CertPrimer 801

ISBN: 978-0-6151-9779-1

About the Author

Randy Smith lives in Omaha, Nebraska with his wife Patty and two sons, Kevin and Eric. He began his Lotus Notes and Domino consulting career in 1996 and founded R.D. Smith Consulting in 2000. Randy is a certified instructor for Lotus Notes and Domino. And, in addition to advanced level certifications in Lotus Notes and Domino Application Development and Systems Administration, he holds certifications in Java, DB2 Universal Database, and WebSphere.

Randy has been developing IT certification practice tests for over five years and was a contributing author for the book *Lotus Notes and Domino 6 System Administrator Exam Cram 2*.

The following is a list of Randy's certifications:

- **IBM Certified Advanced Instructor - Lotus Notes and Domino 8 Application Development**
- IBM Certified Advanced Instructor - Lotus Notes and Domino 8 System Administration
- **IBM Certified Advanced Application Developer - Lotus Notes and Domino 8**
- IBM Certified Advanced System Administrator - Lotus Notes and Domino 8
- IBM Certified Advanced Instructor - Lotus Notes and Domino 7 Application Development
- IBM Certified Advanced Instructor - Lotus Notes and Domino 7 System Administration
- IBM Certified Advanced Application Developer - Lotus Notes and Domino 7
- IBM Certified Advanced System Administrator - Lotus Notes and Domino 7
- IBM Certified Advanced Application Developer - Lotus Notes and Domino 6/6.5
- IBM Certified Advanced System Administrator - Lotus Notes and Domino 6/6.5
- IBM Certified Solution Developer - WebSphere Studio 5
- IBM Certified Database Administrator - DB2 Universal Database 8
- IBM Certified Application Developer - DB2 Universal Database 8
- Sun Certified Programmer for the Java 2 Platform

Contents at a Glance

Table of Contents

Introduction

About CertPrimer Practice Tests

CertPrimer practice tests are handy, affordable resources that can be used to prepare for certification exams. These practice tests are also very useful for assessing your readiness for taking the actual certification exams. Each CertPrimer practice test is developed and reviewed by industry experts who hold certifications in the subject matter.

The format used for the practice test questions is modeled after the actual certification exam. The contents of the practice tests and study aids are based on the list of competencies published in the certification program exam guides.

Who Should Use This Book

The CertPrimer practice tests for *Exam 801: IBM Lotus Notes Domino 8 Application Development Update* are intended for certification candidates who have already earned the certification *IBM Certified Application Developer - Lotus Notes and Domino 7*. By passing Exam 801, the certification candidate will earn the title of *IBM Certified Application Developer - Lotus Notes and Domino 8*.

This book should not be used as your only means for preparing to take the actual certification exam. Hands-on experience with the related products is also very important.

How To Use This Book

CertPrimer practice test books include several study aids to help you prepare for your certification exam. In addition to the practice test questions, CertPrimer also includes flash cards and study notes to reinforce your knowledge of the exam competencies and concepts that you will encounter when you take the actual certification exam.

The certification practice test questions included in this book are broken down by the competency areas, as defined in the certification exam guide published by the Lotus Certification Program. The flash cards are also organized by these competency areas. The study notes provide a quick reference to concepts and information related to the certification exam competencies.

It is recommended that when you take the practice tests included in this book, especially the first time, you should check your answers against the Practice Test Answer Key (Chapter 4) and not the Practice Test Explanations (Chapter 5). This will allow you to identify of any areas of weakness, without associating the text of the correct answers to the questions through memorization. The Answer Key items display only the question number and the letter representing the correct answer. The Explanation items display the full text of the question and correct answer, the related competency area, and references to related product documentation.

Once you've taken the practice tests a few times and have had a chance to assess your strengths and weaknesses in each of the competency areas, take some time to reinforce your knowledge and skills in the areas where you need some help. Review topics in the Lotus Notes and Domino Help databases in areas where you are struggling. And, by all means, go to the related products and try a few things out. Then, with this added confidence, take the practice tests again and start reviewing the explanations associated with the practice test questions.

The flash card items can be used to help you memorize key concepts and information related to the exam competencies. The flash cards have the questions printed on the front with the corresponding answers on the back. You might want to remove the flash card pages from the book, separate them, and carry them around to review them whenever you have a free moment.

The study notes pages contain key information that you will need to know for the certification exam. This information is presented in a concise format, often using bullet points. This format makes it easy to memorize the information. You might also want to remove these pages and carry them around with you to review them at your convenience.

Your comments related to this book are welcomed. Please direct your comments to the author by sending an e-mail to: rsmith@rdsmithconsulting.com

Chapter 1

Certification Path

Certification Requirements

Successfully passing *Exam 801: IBM Lotus Notes Domino 8 Application Development Update* will earn the certification candidate the title of *IBM Certified Application Developer - Lotus Notes and Domino 8*. However, in order to sit for this exam, the candidate must first achieve the certification title of *IBM Certified Application Developer - Lotus Notes and Domino 7*.

Certification Options

In the certification path for IBM Lotus Notes Domino 8 Application Development, there are two methods for achieving the certification title of *IBM Certified Application Developer - Lotus Notes and Domino 8*. These methods are illustrated below:

Method 1

Earn the certification title of *IBM Certified Application Developer - Lotus Notes and Domino 7* and pass the following recertification exam:
- *Exam 801: IBM Lotus Notes Domino 8 Application Development Update*

Method 2

Pass the following three core exams in the IBM Lotus Notes Domino 8 Application Development certification path:
- *Exam 834: IBM Lotus Notes Domino 8 Application Development Foundation Skills*
- *Exam 835: IBM Lotus Notes Domino 8 Application Development Intermediate Skills*
- *Exam 836: IBM Lotus Notes Domino 8 Developing Web Applications*

Chapter 2

Exam Competencies

Competency Areas

Exam 801 contains the following five competency areas:

- Composite Applications
- Design and Development Enhancements
- Domino and DB2 Integration
- Programming Enhancements
- Web Services in Domino Applications

Competency Area 1: Composite Applications

Competency Area 1, *Composite Applications*, contains the following sub-competencies:

- Understand the advantages and structure of composite applications
- Understand and describe the planning process of a composite application
- Understand and describe the creation process of a composite application
- Understand and describe the deployment of a composite application

Competency Area 2: Design and Development Enhancements

Competency Area 2, *Design and Development Enhancements*, contains the following sub-competencies:

- Identify and use new database property settings
  - Allow Compression of Database Design
  - Don't allow simple search
- Identify and use new view indexing options
  - Deferred sort index creation
  - Server-side notes.ini parameter setting: ENABLE_ON_DEMAND_COLLATIONS=1

- Identify and use new view column options
  - Bytes column number format
- Identify and use advanced options for columns
  - Adjust columns for tiled layouts
  - Adjust columns for vertical layouts
  - Extend to use available window width
  - Specify composite application properties
- Utilize "Show default items in right-mouse menu" option
- Utilize "Display as a split button" shared action option
- Manage new agent scheduling options
- Utilize new styles of Rich Text Lite fields

Competency Area 3: Domino and DB2 Integration

Competency Area 3, *Domino and DB2 Integration*, contains the following sub-competencies:

- Understand and use DB2 Access Views
- Understand and use DB2 Query Views
- Identify and use new DB2 Access View fields

Competency Area 4: Programming Enhancements

Competency Area 4, *Programming Enhancements*, contains the following sub-competencies:

- Recognize and use new @Commands as well as new parameters for existing @Commands
  - @Command(FileDatabaseCompact)
  - @Command([CopySelectedAsTable])
  - @Command([CalendarFormat]) 2 work week/1 work month format
- Recognize and use new @Functions as well as new parameters for existing @Functions
  - @GetViewInfo([IsViewFiltered])
  - @URLQueryString
  - @Version (updated)
- Recognize and use new web URL commands and parameters, including:
  - Request_Content_nnn new CGI variable
  - ReadViewEntries URL Option: Endview
  - ReadViewEntries URL Option: Outputformat
- Utilize HTML option control at field and form level

- Identify and use new database templates (dominoblog.ntf, rss_generator.ntf)
- Recognize and use new LotusScript classes, properties, and methods, including:
    - Properties of NotesDXLExporter and NotesDXLImporter
    - NotesDirectory
    - NotesDirectoryNavigator
    - GetProfileDocCollection (profilename parameter is now optional)
    - NotesProperty
    - NotesPropertyBroker
    - NotesDocumentCollection (new methods)
    - NotesView (new methods)
    - NotesUIView Onselect event
    - NotesViewEntryCollection (new methods)
    - OutlineReload
    - Read/Unread Marks Support
    - NotesUIScheduler.DisplayCheckboxes
- Recognize and use new LotusScript language changes
    - Limits on file operations - no line limit on Write statement
- Recognize new Java support features
    - Just-In-Time (JIT) compiler

Competency Area 5: Web Services in Domino Applications

Competency Area 5, *Web Services in Domino Applications*, contains the following sub-competencies:

- Understand combining script libraries for greater efficiency
- Create a Web Service Consumer
- Understand and utilize local preview of Web Services

Chapter 3

Practice Test Questions

About the Practice Tests Questions

The format used for the practice test questions is modeled after the actual certification exam. Each practice test question is a multiple choice question with four possible answers. From the list of possible answers, choose the one that best answers the question.

Competency Area 1: Composite Applications

Question 1

Which type of composite application components are supported in Domino Designer 8?

A. Eclipse components only
B. NSF components only
C. DB2 components only
D. Eclipse and NSF components

Question 2

Which client type is used to launch the Composite Application Editor?

A. Notes 8 Basic Client
B. Notes 8 Standard Client
C. Domino Designer 8 Client
D. Domino Administrator 8 Client

Question 3

What is the name of the managed client software that is used to deploy composite applications hosted on a Domino 8 server?

A. Lotus Expeditor
B. Lotus Integrator
C. Domino Integrator
D. Domino Connect

Question 4

What design elements are available in Domino Designer 8 for composite applications?

A. Wiring Properties and Plug-in Components
B. Applications and Plug-in Components
C. Wiring Properties and Applications
D. Wiring Properties, Applications, and Plug-in Components

Question 5

The Notes 8 Standard Client is based on which of the following frameworks?

A. DB2
B. Eclipse
C. Domino
D. WebSphere

Question 6

Which of the following best describes what a composite application is?

A. An application that combines the presentation, data, and processing layers into a single database
B. An application consisting of multiple design elements from a single Notes database, presented in a frameset
C. An application that combines a user interface and background/scheduled agents to perform a series of tasks
D. An application consisting of a collection of reusable components, from multiple sources, within a service oriented architecture

Question 7

Which composite application design element is used for providing access to WSDL files within a Notes composite application container?

A. WSDL
B. Container
C. Wiring Properties
D. Applications

Question 8

Carolyn assembled a composite application using her Lotus Notes 8 client's Composite Application Editor. In order to access this composite application via a Web browser, where can the composite application be hosted?

A. Domino 8 server only
B. WebSphere Portal 6 server only
C. Domino 7 server or Domino 8 server
D. Domino 8 server or WebSphere Portal 6 server

Question 9

The Composite Application Editor can be used to perform which of the following for composite application components?

A. Add new composite application components
B. Edit composite application components
C. Wire composite application components together
D. All of the above

Question 10

Which of the following best describes Lotus Expeditor?

A. An open-source framework used for extending composite applications to mobile devices
B. A middleware product used for accessing relational data sources, such as DB2, from a Notes 8 application
C. A managed client, based on the Eclipse framework, used for deploying composite applications in a service oriented architecture
D. An integrated development environment, based on the Eclipse framework, that replaces Domino Designer for designing Notes 8 applications

Question 11

An application consisting of a collection of reusable components, from multiple sources, within a service oriented architecture is referred to as what?

A. Component Application
B. Composite Application
C. Web Service Application
D. Service Oriented Application

Question 12

Kelly used the Composite Application Editor to make several changes to the Employee Information composite application hosted on the Domino 8 server CompApps. When will the changes to this composite application take effect?

A. Immediately
B. When the Composite Application Editor is closed
C. When server CompApps is restarted
D. When the Design task runs on server CompApps

Question 13

Which of the following tools is used for assembling and wiring composite applications?

A. Domino Designer Client
B. SOA Application Editor
C. Eclipse Application Editor
D. Composite Application Editor

Question 14

Which of the Lotus Notes and Domino Release 8 client products can be installed as either the basic client or the standard Eclipsed-based client?

A. Lotus Notes client
B. Domino Designer client
C. Domino Administrator client
D. All of the above

Question 15

Which of the following Notes design elements cannot be surfaced as a component in a composite application?

A. Page
B. View
C. Agent
D. Frameset

Question 16

The Composite Application Editor can be used to perform which of the following for a composite application?

A. Modify the application
B. Modify the application pages
C. Modify the application components
D. All of the above

Question 17

The Lotus Notes 8 client software can be installed on a workstation with which of the following configurations?

A. Basic client configuration only
B. Eclipsed-based client configuration only
C. Web browser client configuration only
D. Basic client configuration or Eclipsed-based client configuration

Question 18

A design architecture that uses reusable components and loosely coupled services to support business processes is referred to as what?

A. Service Oriented Application (SOA)
B. Service Oriented Architecture (SOA)
C. Component Services Architecture (CSA)
D. Web Services Architecture (WSA)

Question 19

Which of the following steps should be performed first when creating a new Notes 8 composite application container using the Notes 8 client?

A. Select "File > Application > New" and choose the "-Blank Composite Application-" template
B. Select "File > Application > New", choose the "-Blank-" template, and in the Launch tab of the Database Properties select "Launch as Composite Application"
C. Select "File > Application > Composite Application Editor" and then select the "New Application Container" action button in the Composite Application Editor
D. Select "Tools > Composite Application Editor" and then select "File > New > Composite Application Container" in the Composite Application Editor

Question 20

The Property Broker Editor contains tabs to define each of the following, except:

A. Type
B. Action
C. Schema
D. Property

Question 21

Notes 8 composite applications can reside on which of the following?

A. Domino 8 server
B. WebSphere Portal 6 server
C. Local machine of a Lotus Notes 8 client
D. All of the above

Question 22

Dale wants to ensure that the elements and attributes in his WSDL files are treated as unique names by the composite applications editor. Which of the following should he do?

A. Use Namespaces in the WSDL file
B. Use the <Unique> identifier for all elements and attributes in the WDSL file
C. Use the <UniqueID> identifier for all elements and attributes in the WDSL file
D. Create separate WSDL files whenever duplicate elements or attributes are required

Question 23

Which of the following statements regarding Notes composite application components is false?

A. A single Notes database can contain multiple components for a composite application
B. A Notes component can be used in multiple composite applications
C. Composite applications consisting of Notes components can be hosted on Domino servers running Release 7.02 or later
D. Composite applications consisting of Notes components can be hosted on WebSphere Portal servers running release 6.0 or later

Question 24

Which of the following best describes Eclipse?

A. A proprietary framework developed by IBM, used for extending Notes 8 applications to mobile devices
B. An integrated development environment that replaces Domino Designer for designing Notes 8 applications
C. A middleware product used for accessing relational data sources, such as DB2, from a Notes 8 application
D. An open-source framework used for creating integrated development environments and deploying rich client applications

Question 25

Where is the composite application wiring panel located?

A. Composite Application Editor
B. Component Wiring Editor
C. Domino Designer Client
D. Domino Administrator Client

Question 26

Which of the following statements regarding the Lotus Notes 8 basic and standard client configurations is false?

A. The Lotus Notes 8 standard client is built on the Eclipse framework
B. Applications accessed from the Lotus Notes 8 standard client must use the optional DB2 data store

C. The Lotus Notes 8 standard client configuration can run composite applications, but the basic client configuration cannot

D. Some Lotus Notes and Domino design features that work in the standard client configuration will not work in the basic client configuration

Question 27

Which composite application design element is used for providing access to the XML files that contain composite application definitions for a Notes composite application?

A. Container
B. XML Descriptor
C. Wiring Properties
D. Applications

Question 28

What does the acronym XML represent?

A. Extended Machine Language
B. Executable Machine Language
C. Extensible Markup Language
D. Executable Markup Language

Question 29

Design elements of Lotus Notes databases used in a composite applications are known as what?

A. NSF Components
B. WSDL Components
C. Eclipse Components
D. Web Service Components

Question 30

Which of the following best describes the Notes 8 Standard Client architecture?

A. Notes 8 Standard Client is built on the Lotus Expeditor framework, which is built on the Eclipse framework
B. Notes 8 Standard Client is built on the Eclipse framework, which is built on the Lotus Expeditor framework
C. Notes 8 Standard Client is built on the WebSphere Portal framework, which is built on the Eclipse framework
D. Notes 8 Standard Client is built on the Lotus Expeditor framework, which is built on the WebSphere Portal framework

Question 31

What does the acronym SOA represent?

A. Service Oriented Application
B. Service Oriented Architecture
C. Simple Object Architecture
D. Single Object Application

Question 32

The "Launch as Composite Application" option in the Launch tab of the Database Properties would work best in which of the following scenarios?

A. All users of the application will be running the Lotus Notes 8 Basic client
B. All users of the application will be running the Lotus Notes 8 Standard client
C. Users of the application will be a mix of Lotus Notes 7 and Lotus Notes 8 clients
D. You have created outline entries that open to different pages of a composite application

Question 33

Which of the following statements regarding the publishing of properties by NSF components is true?

A. The LotusScript API can be used to publish properties
B. Folder columns can be used to publish properties
C. View columns can be used to publish properties
D. All of the above

Question 34

Which of the following is a true statement regarding the properties of a composite application component?

A. A component can publish properties but cannot consume properties
B. A component can consume properties but cannot publish properties
C. A component can consume properties, publish properties, or both
D. A component can either consume properties or publish properties, but not both

Question 35

Which of the following tools is used for creating and editing the WSDL files for the Composite Application Properties design elements?

A. WSDL Editor
B. Property Broker Editor
C. SOA Application Editor
D. Composite Application Editor

Question 36

Which of the following can be used to build components for a composite application?

A. Domino Designer 8
B. Rational Application Developer
C. An Eclipse IDE
D. All of the above

Question 37

Which of the follow describes how the Property Broker Editor is launched?

A. Select "Tools > Property Broker Editor" from the Lotus Notes 8 client
B. Select "Tools > Property Broker Editor" from the Domino Designer 8 client
C. Open a composite application in the Domino Designer 8 client, select a Property design element from the "Composite Applications > Properties" design list, and select "Actions > Edit Property"
D. Open a composite application in the Domino Designer 8 client, select a Property design element from the "Composite Applications > Properties" design list, and select the "Open File" action button

Question 38

Pete has created several composite application components. In order to assemble these components in a composite application for the Lotus Notes 8 client, which of the following best describes the steps to be followed?

A. First, create a Lotus Notes composite application container. Next, add the components to the composite application container. Finally, wire the components together
B. First, create a Lotus Notes composite application container. Next, wire the components together. Finally, add the components to the composite application container
C. First, add the components to the composite application. Next, wire the components together. Finally, create a Lotus Notes composite application container
D. First, add the components to the composite application. Next, create a Lotus Notes composite application container. Finally, wire the components together

Question 39

Which of the following describes how an NSF component of a composite application can consume a property of another component?

A. This is not possible. NSF components may only publish properties. They cannot consume properties.
B. In the Advanced tab of the Action Properties of an action in the Notes design element, select the WSDL action that is wired to receive the property

C. In the Advanced tab of the Database Properties associated with the NSF component, select the WSDL action that is wired to receive the property

D. In the Advanced tab of the Composite Application Properties associated with the NSF component, select the WSDL action that is wired to receive the property

Question 40

Which of the follow describes how the Composite Application Editor is launched?

A. Select "Tools > Composite Application Editor" from the Lotus Notes 8 client
B. Select "Tools > Composite Application Editor" from the Domino Designer 8 client
C. Open a composite application in the Lotus Notes 8 client and select "Actions > Edit Application"
D. Open a composite application in the Domino Designer 8 client and select "Actions > Edit Application"

Question 41

Pat has created a frameset to open an application as a composite application to the Welcome page. This frameset is specified in the "Open designated Frameset" option in the Launch tab of the Database Properties. What will occur if a user running the Lotus Notes 7 client opens this application?

A. The Lotus Notes 7 client will crash
B. The error message "Invalid NSF version" will be displayed and the application will not open
C. The error message "Invalid NSF version" will be displayed and the application will open to the default view
D. The Composite Application settings configured in the Frameset Properties will be ignored and the application will open to the designated frameset

Question 42

The Property Broker Editor feature of the Domino Designer 8 uses which of the following to define properties, types, and actions?

A. WSDL
B. Java
C. LotusScript
D. JavaScript

Question 43

Which of the following will occur when a new composite application container is created from the Notes 8 "-Blank Composite Application-" template?

A. The Property Broker Editor will be launched
B. The Composite Application Editor will be launched

C. A page will be displayed in the Notes client indicating that the application does not contain any content
D. All of the above

Question 44

Which of the following methods can be used to create a new Notes 8 composite application?

A. Create the composite application from the Notes 8 "-Blank Composite Application-" template
B. Open an existing Notes 8 application in Domino Designer 8 and select the "New Application" action button in the Composite Application design list
C. Open an existing Notes 8 application in Domino Designer 8, select the "Import XML" action button in the Composite Application design list, and select an existing composite application XML file to import
D. All of the above

Competency Area 2: Design and Development Enhancements

Question 1

What is the purpose of the "Show default items in right mouse menu" setting in the Action Bar properties?

A. Display or hide system default actions in the right-click menu for forms
B. Display or hide system default actions in the right-click menu for views and folders
C. Display or hide system default actions in the right-click menu for forms, views, and folders
D. Highlight the right-click menu actions and sub-actions that were designated as the default actions

Question 2

Which of following statements regarding split button actions is true?

A. Only the parent action of a sub-action can be defined as a split button
B. When users click on the left side of a split button, the first sub-action will be executed
C. When users click on the down arrow on the right side of a split button, a list of sub-actions will be displayed as a drop-down menu
D. All of the above

Question 3

What is the purpose of the "Extend to use available window width" setting in the Advanced tab of the Column Properties?

A. Allows users to manually resize any column in the view
B. Allows users to manually resize the last column in the view
C. Automatically expands any column in the view to fill the width of the viewable window
D. Automatically expands the last column in the view to fill the width of the viewable window

Question 4

If the AnnualSales field contains the value 1,500,000 how will this field be displayed in a view column with the number format of Bytes(K/M/G)?

A. 1M
B. 1.4M
C. 1.5M
D. 1.5K

Question 5

Which of the following view features are available in the Lotus Notes 8 standard client configuration?

A. Tiled Views
B. Narrow Views
C. Partial Response Hierarchies
D. All of the above

Question 6

Randy added a Rich Text Lite field to a form to include small thumbnail images of screenshots. The Thumbnail option was chosen in the "Limit Input > Only allow" property. However, when a user adds a screenshot image to this field, the image is displayed in its original size. What could Randy do to ensure that these thumbnail images are displayed in a small, uniform size?

A. Resize the image programmatically by adding an Input Translation Formula to the Rich Text Lite field
B. Enable the "Resize Thumbnail Image, in pixels" property for the Rich Text Lite field, and enter the desired width and height
C. Add instructions to the form, requesting users to resize the thumbnail images to the desired size before saving the document
D. Place the Rich Text Lite field in a Table and set the table cell properties to a fixed width and height for the desired thumbnail size

Question 7

Eric is creating a new view in a database. Several of the columns in the view have been set up as user-sorted columns. What can Eric do to minimize the server performance impact related to the user-sorted columns?

A. Enable the View property "Defer index creation until first use"
B. Disable the View property "Defer index creation until first use"
C. Enable the Column property "Defer index creation until first use" for each user-sorted column in the view
D. Disable the Column property "Defer index creation until first use" for each user-sorted column in the view

Question 8

Kevin is designing a view that includes a column that displays the value of the "Comments" field. He would like to have this column automatically expanded to fill the width of the viewable window. How can he accomplish this?

A. The Comments column must be the first column in the view, and the Column/Style property "Resize to window width" must be enabled
B. The Comments column must be the last column in the view, and the View/Style property "Extend last column to window width" must be enabled

C. The Comments column must be the last column in the view, and the View/Style property "Extend last column to window width" must be disabled

D. The Comments column may be any column in the view, and the Column/Advanced property "Extend to use available window width" must be enabled

Question 9

The following statements regarding the "Bytes(K/M/G)" number format in view columns are true, except?

A. The size of the number determines the suffix that is displayed
B. Kilobyte values are displayed as whole numbers
C. Megabyte and Gigabyte values are displayed with one decimal place
D. Terabyte values are displayed using scientific notation

Question 10

When a view is displayed as a narrow view, how many rows can be displayed for each entry?

A. Only one row per entry can be displayed
B. Up to two rows per entry will be displayed, depending on the settings in the Column Properties
C. Up to nine rows per entry will be displayed, depending on the settings in the View Properties
D. An unlimited number of rows per entry will be displayed, depending on the width of the narrow view

Question 11

Which of the following is not a valid agent event trigger?

A. Before new mail arrives
B. After new mail arrives
C. When database is opened
D. When server starts

Question 12

Which of the following property settings will add information fields to new documents in a database, enabling them to be sorted into a document response hierarchy?

A. The "Support Response Thread History" setting in the Advanced tab of the Form Properties
B. The "Support Response Thread History" setting in the Advanced tab of the View Properties
C. The "Support Response Thread History" setting in the Advanced tab of the Document Properties
D. The "Support Response Thread History" setting in the Advanced tab of the Database Properties

Question 13

Patty is redesigning the "Employee Info" form to display a fixed-sized, thumbnail image of the employee's photo. Which of the following methods bests describes how this can be accomplished?

A. Create a Rich Text field on the form and open the Control tab of the Field properties. Select "Thumbnail" in the "Only allow" property, enable the "Resize Thumbnail Image in pixels" property and enter the desired width and height in pixels.
B. Create a Rich Text Lite field on the form and open the Control tab of the Field properties. Select "Thumbnail" in the "Only allow" property, enable the "Resize Thumbnail Image in pixels" property and enter the desired width and height in pixels.
C. Create a Thumbnail Image field on the form and open the Control tab of the Field properties. Enable the "Resize Thumbnail Image in pixels" property and enter the desired width and height in pixels.
D. Create a Thumbnail Image field on the form and open the Control tab of the Field properties. Enable the "Resize Thumbnail Image on import" property, choose either inches or pixels and enter the desired width and height.

Question 14

Users of the Projects.nsf database are indicating that they are unable to use the right-click menu in the Active Projects view to display the Document Properties dialog box for the view entries. What could be causing this behavior?

A. The hide/when property of the "Document Properties" default system action is evaluating to True
B. The hide/when property of the "Document Properties" default system action is evaluating to False
C. The Action Bar property "Show default items in right mouse menu" has been enabled
D. The Action Bar property "Show default items in right mouse menu" has been disabled

Question 15

Robyn, a Domino developer, would like to create a split button action in the Help Desk application. For which client types will the split button feature work?

A. Notes 7.02 Client and later
B. Notes 8 Basic Client only
C. Notes 8 Standard Client only
D. Notes 8 Basic client and Notes 8 Standard Client

Question 16

Which of the following represent all of the valid suffixes that can be displayed in a view column using the "Bytes(K/M/G)" number format?

A. K, M, G
B. K, M, G, T
C. KB, MB, GB
D. Bytes, Kilobytes. Megabytes, Gigabytes

Question 17

Which of the following best represents the viewers that can be specified in the "Viewers:" setting in the Options tab of the View Properties dialog box?

A. Standard and Calendar viewers only
B. Vertical and Horizontal viewers only
C. Standard and Narrow viewers only
D. Table, Tiled, Calendar, and third party viewers

Question 18

Ron created the BuildProfiles agent in the AppStats.nsf database. He runs this agent manually each time that he restarts the Apps1 server. He would like to automate the execution of this agent. How would he do this?

A. Add "AppStats.nsf:BuildProfiles" to the RunAtStartup Notes.INI variable on server Apps1
B. Add "BuildProfiles:AppStats.nsf" to the RunAtStartup Notes.INI variable on server Apps1
C. In the Runtime section of the Agent Properties, select "On schedule" for the Agent Trigger and select the "When server starts" option
D. In the Runtime section of the Agent Properties, select "On event" for the Agent Trigger and select the "When server starts" option

Question 19

Which of the following property settings will disable searches from the Search Bar in the Lotus Notes client when a database is not full-text indexed?

A. Disable the setting "Allow database search" in the Advanced tab of the Database Properties
B. Enable the setting "Don't allow database search" in the Advanced tab of the Database Properties
C. Enable the setting "Don't allow simple search" in the Advanced tab of the Database Properties
D. Disable the setting "Don't allow simple search" in the Advanced tab of the Database Properties

Question 20

What is the purpose of the Thumbnail option in the Control tab of the Field Properties dialog box?

A. To display a fixed size image in a Rich Text field
B. To display a fixed size image in a Rich Text Lite field

C. To display a fixed size image in a field within a table cell
D. To display an image in a view column that represents the field's contents

Question 21

What does the acronym ODS represent?

A. Object Delivery System
B. Object Delivery Service
C. Open Domain Server
D. On-Disk Structure

Question 22

If the TotalCalls field contains the value 250, how will this field be displayed in a view column with the number format of Bytes(K/M/G)?

A. 0K
B. 1K
C. 0.2K
D. 0.25K

Question 23

If the BilledHours field contains the value 1,200, how will this field be displayed in a view column with the number format of Bytes(K/M/G)?

A. 1K
B. 1.1K
C. 1.2K
D. 1.17K

Question 24

Which of following statements regarding split button actions is false?

A. Split buttons are only available for view and folder actions
B. Only the parent action of a sub-action can be defined as a split button
C. The icon display settings are disabled in the Action Properties when an action is configured as a split button
D. When used from a Notes 8 Basic client, an action button configured as a split button will not provide the split button functionality

Question 25

Which On Disk Structure (ODS) version can a database use in order to take advantage of the Design Note Compression feature?

A. ODS 43 only
B. ODS 45 only
C. ODS 48 only
D. ODS 45 or ODS 48

Question 26

Which of the following features requires the optional On Disk Structure (ODS) version 48?

A. Enhanced user activity detail (adds, updates and deletes)
B. Design Note Compression (for reducing I/O and database size)
C. User Rename List stored in database (for changes to Reader Name and Author Name fields)
D. All of the above

Question 27

Marcia would like to defer the creation of indexes for user-sorted columns in the views of Projects.nsf database. Where would she go to make this change?

A. Enable the setting "Defer index creation until first use" in the Sorting tab of the View Properties dialog box
B. Enable the setting "Defer index creation until first use" in the Sorting tab of the Database Properties dialog box
C. Enable the setting "Defer index creation until first use" in the Advanced tab of the View Properties dialog box
D. Enable the setting "Defer index creation until first use" in the Sorting tab of the Column Properties dialog box for the user-sorted columns

Question 28

Which of the following represents the choices available for the Column Properties setting "If view is narrow"?

A. Keep on top, Hide this column, Wrap to second row
B. Keep on top, Wrap to second row, Tile view entries
C. Wrap to second row, Hide this column, Tile view entries
D. Tile view entries, Wrap to second row, Extend to window width

Question 29

The Description column is the first column displayed in the Products view. How could the Description column be configured so that it will automatically be expanded to fill the width of the viewable window?

A. In the Style tab of the View Properties dialog box, enable the setting "Extend first column to window width"
B. In the Style tab of the View Properties dialog box, enable the setting "Resize to window width" and enter "0' for the "Column number" setting

C. In the Style tab of the View Properties dialog box, enable the setting "Resize to window width" and enter "1' for the "Column number" setting
D. In the Advanced tab of the Column Properties for the Description column, enable the setting "Extend to use available window width"

Question 30

What is the purpose of the "Viewers:" setting in the Options tab of the View Properties dialog box?

A. To specify Table, Tiled, Calendar, and third party viewers that users of composite applications can switch between
B. To specify a list of names and groups that are allowed to access the view from any Lotus Notes client configuration
C. To specify a list of names and groups that are allowed to access the view from a Lotus Notes 8 basic client configuration
D. To specify a list of names and groups that are allowed to access the view from a Lotus Notes 8 standard client configuration

Question 31

Tara has created several actions in the Projects view that are available in the right-click menu. These are the only actions that users need in the right-click menu for this view. Since the system and default view actions are also displayed in the right-click menu, users must look to the bottom of a long list of menu choices to find the custom view actions. What can Tara do to make these custom view actions more accessible to the users?

A. In the Action Bar properties, enable the property "Show default items in right mouse menu"
B. In the Action Bar properties, disable the property "Show default items in right mouse menu"
C. In the Action properties for each action, enable the property "Show before default items"
D. In the Action properties for each action, disable the property "Show before default items"

Question 32

Which of the following is a characteristic of the Narrow View feature?

A. Narrow views have a vertical orientation
B. Narrow views are only available in the standard client configuration
C. A view column can be configured so that it is hidden only when displayed in a narrow view
D. All of the above

Question 33

Which of the following statements is true, regarding the "Bytes(K/M/G)" number format in view columns?

A. The values displayed in the column are rounded to the nearest number, but never less than 1K
B. When the "Bytes(K/M/G)" number format is selected, a display suffix must also be selected
C. Only one display suffix (K, M, or G) may be selected for displaying all of the numbers in the column
D. All of the above

Question 34

What is the purpose of the "When server starts" agent trigger option in the Agent Properties?

A. This is an "On schedule" trigger that stops and restarts the Domino server
B. This is an "On schedule" trigger that stops and restarts the Agent Manager (AMGR) server task
C. This is an "On event" trigger that executes the agent each time the Domino server is started
D. This is an "On schedule" trigger that executes the agent each time the Domino server is started

Question 35

Which of the following best describes the purpose of the Notes.ini variable "Designer_ShowPropForJavaViewsUI"?

A. When enabled on a developer's machine, certain design properties, available only for the Lotus Notes standard client configuration, are displayed in the Domino Designer client.
B. When enabled on a developer's machine, certain design properties, available only for the Lotus Notes basic client configuration, are displayed in the Domino Designer client.
C. When disabled on a user's machine with the Lotus Notes standard client configuration, certain composite applications features will no longer be available to the user.
D. When disabled on a user's machine with the Lotus Notes basic client configuration, certain composite applications features will no longer be available to the user.

Question 36

Which of the following statements is true regarding the "Don't allow simple search" setting in the Advanced tab of the Database Properties?

A. When this setting is enabled, the Search Bar icon in the Lotus Notes client will be disabled
B. When this setting is enabled, the full-text index for the database will be deleted and users will be prevented from creating a full-text index
C. When this setting is enabled, the "Find text in document" search function for documents and the "Starts with..." search function for views will be disabled
D. When this setting is enabled, an error message will be displayed if a user attempts to perform a search from the Search Bar in the Lotus Notes client when the database is not full-text indexed

Question 37

Which of the following is not a valid option in the "Notes using the Eclipse-base UI" section of the Options tab in the View Properties dialog box?

A. Hide the column header
B. Show partial response hierarchies
C. Show Vertical/Horizontal switcher
D. Extend to use available window width

Question 38

What is the purpose of the setting "Don't allow simple search" in the Advanced tab of the Database Properties?

A. To prevent searches against a database that is not full-text indexed
B. To prevent "Starts with..." searches when a view is being displayed
C. To prevent "Find text in document" searches when a document is being displayed
D. All of the above

Question 39

Matt would like to have the second row of the Projects view indented when displayed as a narrow view. Which of the following represents the best way for him to accomplish this?

A. On the Style tab of the View Properties, choose the setting "If view is narrow: Justify second row"
B. On the Advanced tab of the Column Properties for a column in the view, choose the setting "If view is narrow: Justify second row"
C. On the Advanced tab of the Column Properties for a column in the view, choose the setting "If view is narrow: Wrap to second row" and enable the setting "Indent this column"
D. On the Advanced tab of the Column Properties for a column in the view, choose the setting "If view is narrow: Keep on top" and enable the setting "Justify second row under this column"

Question 40

Which of the following statements is true, regarding the Thumbnail option in a Rich Text Lite field?

A. A fixed height and width can be defined for the thumbnail image
B. If the Thumbnail option is selected, an image attachment name must be included
C. When the Thumbnail option is selected, all other selections will automatically be deselected
D. All of the above

Question 41

What is the purpose of the "Display as a split button" setting in the Action Properties dialog box?

A. Displays all sub-actions associated with the action button as separate action buttons.
B. Allows users to execute the first sub-action action associated with the action button by clicking on the left side of the button or display the list of sub-actions by clicking on the down arrow on the right side of the button.
C. Allows users to execute the first sub-action action associated with the action button by clicking on the right side of the button or display the list of sub-actions by clicking on the down arrow on the left side of the button.
D. Allows a default sub-action setting to be selected. This allows users to execute the default sub-action action associated with the action button by clicking on the left side of the button or display the list of sub-actions by clicking on the down arrow on the right side of the button.

Question 42

What Notes.ini variable is required in order to make the setting "Display separator above this entry" available in the Outline Entry Properties dialog box?

A. Designer_ShowPropForJavaViewsUI=1
B. Designer_ShowPropForJavaViewsUI=0
C. Designer_ShowPropForJavaViewsUI="Standard"
D. Designer_ShowPropForJavaViewsUI="Basic"

Question 43

What is the purpose of the setting "Support Response Thread History" in the Advanced tab of the Database Properties?

A. Displays the entire document response hierarchy whenever a parent document is displayed in a view
B. Adds information fields to new documents in a database, enabling them to be sorted into a document response hierarchy
C. Adds information fields to existing documents in a database, enabling them to be sorted into a document response hierarchy
D. Adds information fields to new and existing documents in a database, enabling them to be sorted into a document response hierarchy

Question 44

Which of the following statements is true, regarding the "Bytes(K/M/G)" number format in view columns?

A. Kilobytes are displayed with the suffix "K"
B. Values are truncated to display whole numbers only

C. A number less than 1 Kilobyte (1024 Bytes) will be displayed as the actual number, in decimal format

D. All of the above

Question 45

Brenda would like to create a split button for an action in the Customers view. However, the setting "Display as a split button" is not being shown in the Action Properties dialog box. What might be causing this?

A. Split button actions are only available for Form actions
B. The Notes.ini variable "Designer_ShowPropForJavaViewsUI" is missing
C. The setting "Display as a split button" is an Action Bar property, not an individual Action property
D. The Domino Designer 8 Basic client is being used and this property is only available in the Domino Designer 8 Standard client

Question 46

Which of the following statements is true, regarding the horizontal separator feature for Outlines?

A. The setting "Display separator above this entry" in the Outline Entry Properties must be enabled in order to display a horizontal separator
B. The Notes.ini file must include the variable "Designer_ShowPropForJavaViewsUI=1" in order to enable the setting for a horizontal separator
C. Only users with the Notes 8 Standard client will see the horizontal separators in the Outline
D. All of the above

Question 47

Since the HelpDesk.nsf database is extremely large, Jim would like to prevent searches against the databases. Which of the following would allow him to do this?

A. In the Full-Text tab of the Database Properties, click on the "Delete Index..." action
B. In the Full-Text tab of the Database Properties, enable the setting "Don't allow simple search"
C. In the Advanced tab of the Database Properties, enable the setting "Don't allow simple search"
D. In the Advanced tab of the Database Properties, disable the setting "Don't allow simple search"

Question 48

What is the purpose of the "Defer index creation until first use" setting in the Sorting tab of the Column Properties?

A. To defer the creation of the full-text index for a view until a user clicks on the "Create Index..." action button to the left of the column headings
B. To defer the creation of the full-text index for a view until a user clicks on the "Sort..." action button to the right of the column headings
C. To defer the creation of the full-text index for a view until a user clicks on the "Sort..." action button to the left of the column headings
D. To defer the creation of the sort index for a user-sorted column until a user clicks on the column header to re-sort the view

Question 49

When a view is displayed as a narrow view, what determines which columns are displayed on the first row and which columns are displayed on the second row?

A. Only one column can be designated as the first row column by choose the setting "If view is narrow: Keep on top" in the Advanced tab of the Column Properties. All other columns will automatically be displayed on the second row.
B. Multiple columns can be designated as first row columns by choose the setting "If view is narrow: Keep on top" in the Advanced tab of the Column Properties. Columns can be designated as second row columns by choose the setting "If view is narrow: Wrap to second row" in the Advanced tab of the Column Properties.
C. Only one column can be designated as the first row column by entering the column number in the setting "Column to display on top if view is narrow:" in the Advanced tab of the Column Properties. All other columns will automatically be displayed on the second row.
D. Multiple columns can be designated as first row columns by entering the column numbers in the setting "Column(s) to display on top if view is narrow:" in the Advanced tab of the Column Properties. All other columns will automatically be displayed on the second row.

Question 50

Which of the following represents the choices available for the Column Properties setting "For Tile Viewer"?

A. Display on top, Display on bottom, Hide this column
B. Display on top, Display on bottom, Wrap to second row
C. Display on top, Display on bottom, Extend to window width
D. Keep on top, Wrap to second row, Extend to window width

Question 51

Which of the following statements regarding the "Support Response Thread History" setting is true?

A. This setting impacts new documents only
B. This setting is located in the Advanced Tab of the Database Properties dialog box
C. The field $TUA is added to documents to enable them to be sorted into a response hierarchy
D. All of the above

Competency Area 3: Domino and DB2 Integration

Question 1

What does the acronym DAV represent in a Notes database?

A. Domain Authorization View
B. Domino Access View
C. Distributed Access View
D. DB2 Access View

Question 2

Which of the following DB2 Access View (DAV) special fields allow developers to create functions that can use information related to the location of the Notes database containing the DAV?

A. $Server and $Database
B. #Server and #Database
C. #Server, #Filepath, and #DBName
D. $Server, $Filepath, and $Database

Question 3

Andy would like to verify that the Notes database he is currently accessing is DB2-enabled. How could he do this?

A. Look for the message "Database is DB2 Enabled" at the bottom of the Info tab of the Database Properties
B. Ensure that the checkbox "DB2 Enabled" is checked in the Design tab of the Database Properties
C. Ensure that the checkbox "NSFDB2" is checked in the Advanced tab of the Database Properties
D. The filename extension for the database will be ".DB2" instead of ".NSF"

Question 4

Which of the following design elements is a shared resource that enables developers to define DB2 views of data within a DB2-enabled Notes database?

A. Query Access View (QAV)
B. SQL Query View (SQV)
C. DB2 Access View (DAV)
D. DB2 Table View (DTV)

Question 5

Which of the following DB2 Access View (DAV) special fields allow developers to create DB2 Query Views containing response hierarchies?

A. $Ref and $Descendants
B. #Ref and #Descendants
C. #Ref and #RespInfo
D. #Parent and #Children

Question 6

Which of the following statements regarding DB2-enabled Notes databases is true?

A. Domino stores the NSF as a set of DB2 tables
B. A DB2 Access View must be created and populated to expose the NSF data via a DB2 Query View
C. The selection criteria for a DB2 Query Views uses SQL query statements
D. All of the above

Question 7

Which of the following statements regarding the naming of a new DB2 Access View (DAV) in Domino Designer is true?

A. The name of a DAV must be all lower case
B. The prefix "dav_" will be appended to the DAV name when the DAV is saved
C. If spaces are entered in the DAV name, they will be converted to underscores when the DAV is saved
D. All of the above

Question 8

Gretchen ran the following SQL statement against the DB2 Access View "DAV_ByDept":

```
DELETE from DAV_ByDept where DEPT = 'SALES'
```

This SQL statement failed after processing only 10 of the 25 rows that contained "SALES" in the DEPT column. What will be the impact of running this SQL statement?

A. The 10 rows that were processed before the failure will be deleted
B. Since the operation did not complete successfully, the entire operation is rolled back and no rows will be deleted
C. The 10 rows that were processed before the failure will have delete stubs created and the remaining rows will remain unchanged
D. The 10 rows that were processed before the failure will be deleted and delete stubs will be created for the remaining rows that were not processed

Question 9

Colleen created a new DAV design element and notices a yellow triangle icon with an exclamation point beside the DAV name in the DB2 Access Views design list. What does this icon indicate?

A. An error occurred during the creation of the DAV
B. The DAV was successfully created and populated in DB2
C. The DAV was successfully created in DB2 and is now ready to be populated
D. The DAV design element was successfully created and is now ready to be created and populated in DB2

Question 10

Which of the following statements regarding SQL transaction processing against DB2 Access Views is true?

A. Bulk Update transactions are committed as a single transaction. If the operation fails before all rows are updated, the entire transaction is rolled back and no rows will be updated.
B. Bulk Delete transactions are processed as individual transactions. If the operation fails before all rows are processed, only the rows that were processed before the failure will be deleted.
C. Bulk Insert transactions are processed as individual transactions. If the operation fails before all rows are processed, only the rows that were processed before the failure will be inserted.
D. All of the above

Question 11

Dan created a new DB2 Access View (DAV) in the HelpDesk.nsf database. In Domino Designer, he notices a green check mark icon beside the DAV name in the DB2 Access Views design list. What does this icon indicate?

A. An error occurred during the creation of the DAV
B. The DAV was successfully created and populated in DB2
C. The DAV was successfully created in DB2 and is now ready to be populated
D. The DAV design element was successfully created and is now ready to be created and populated in DB2

Question 12

What does the acronym SQL represent?

A. Structured Query Language
B. System Query Language
C. System Query Library
D. Structured Query Log

Question 13

A DB2 Query View can be created to display which of the following?

A. Notes data only
B. Federated data only
C. A combination of Notes data and federated data
D. All of the above

Question 14

The following statements regarding DB2 Query Views are true, except?

A. DB2 Query Views are dynamic
B. A DB2 Query View uses SQL to populate its data
C. Federated data documents can be opened from a DB2 Query View
D. A DB2 Query View can be created to display a combination of Notes documents and federated data documents

Competency Area 4: Programming Enhancements

Question 1

Which of the following can be used to determine if the @SetViewInfo function was used to filter documents from a view?

A. @IsViewFiltered
B. @GetViewFilter
C. @GetViewInfo([IsViewFiltered])
D. @GetViewFilter([IsViewFiltered])

Question 2

Which of the following can be used to populate a NotesViewEntryCollection with the documents in a view that have been unread by the current user?

A. The UnreadEntries property of the NotesView class
B. The GetAllUnreadEntries method of the NotesView class
C. The UnreadEntries property of the NotesViewEntryCollection class
D. The GetUnreadEntries method of the NotesViewEntryCollection class

Question 3

Which LotusScript class is used to handle communications between Composite Application components?

A. NotesPropertyBroker
B. NotesCompositeApplication
C. NotesApplicationContainer
D. NotesApplicationCollection

Question 4

Java support in Notes 8 includes which of the following?

A. Ability to use Java 5 syntax
B. Improved garbage collection
C. Just-In-Time compiler
D. All of the above

Question 5

Which LotusScript class is used to perform lookups of a Notes directory?

A. NotesNameLookup
B. NotesDirectoryLookup

C. NotesDirectoryNavigator
D. NotesNameDirectoryLookup

Question 6

Which of the following statements regarding the NotesDirectory class in LotusScript is true?

A. A NotesDirectory object can be used to represent a Notes directory on a local machine
B. A NotesDirectory object can be used to represent a Notes directory on a Domino server
C. A NotesDirectory object is associated with one or more directory navigators
D. All of the above

Question 7

The Comments rich text field of a document contains four paragraphs of text with 40 characters in each paragraph. What would the function @AbstractSimple("Comments") return for this document?

A. A single text string containing all of the text included in the Comments field
B. A single text string containing the text of the first two paragraphs of the Comments field
C. A single text string containing all of the text of the first two paragraphs plus 20 characters of the third paragraph of the Comments field
D. A text list of four elements, with each element containing the text of a single paragraph of the Comments field

Question 8

Which of the following can be used to create a NotesNoteCollection of all documents in a database that have been read by the current user?

A. The ReadDocuments property of the NotesDatabase class
B. The AllReadDocuments property of the NotesDatabase class
C. The GetAllReadDocuments method of the NotesDatabase class
D. The GetAllReadDocuments method of the NotesDocumentCollection class

Question 9

Which LotusScript class is used for representing a property in a Composite Application?

A. NotesProperty
B. NotesPropertyBroker
C. NotesCompositeProperty
D. NotesApplicationProperty

Question 10

The CalendarFormat @Command can be used to display a calendar view in each of the following formats, except:

A. One work week
B. Two work weeks
C. One work month
D. One work year

Question 11

Tom is creating a LotusScript agent to export documents in the HelpDesk.nsf database to DXL. He wishes to exclude any rich text field attachments from the DXL output. How can he best accomplish this?

A. Set the NotesDXLExporter.OmitRichtextAttachments property to False
B. Set the NotesDXLExporter.OmitRichtextAttachments property to True
C. After the documents have been exported, run an agent to search for and remove all <attachment> tags
D. After the documents have been exported, run an agent to search for and remove all <richtext_attachment> tags

Question 12

What does the acronym DXL represent?

A. Domino XML
B. Domain Execution List
C. Domain Execution Language
D. Domino Extension Language

Question 13

Which of the following can be used to copy selected view entries as a table to the clipboard?

A. @Command([CopySelectedAsTable])
B. @CopySelected(server : database; view; "Table")
C. @CopySelected([TABLE]; server : database; view)
D. @CopySelectedAsTable(server : database; view)

Question 14

Gene would like to construct a URL that ensures that the last entry returned from a ReadViewEntries URL command is the last entry in a view. Which of the following URL commands should he use?

A. ReadViewEntries=Endview
B. ReadViewEntries&Endview=0
C. ReadViewEntries&Endview=1
D. ReadViewEntries&Endview=Last

Question 15

Helena would like to construct a URL that will navigate the rows of a view in reverse order. Which of the following URL commands should she use?

A. ReadViewEntries=NavigateReverse
B. ReadViewEntries&Navigate=Last
C. ReadViewEntries&Navigate=Reverse
D. ReadViewEntries&NavigateReverse=1

Question 16

The following statements regarding the RichTextOption property of the NotesDXLExporter class are true, except:

A. The RICHTEXTOPTION_DXL option exports rich text data as a <richtext> element in normal DXL format
B. The RICHTEXTOPTION_RAW option exports rich text data as a <rawdataitem> element, encoded in Base64
C. The RICHTEXTOPTION_RAW option (an integer value of 1) is the default value for this property
D. If rich text data is exported with the RICHTEXTOPTION_RAW option, importing the data with NotesDXLImporter will import the data exactly the same as the original data

Question 17

Fran is defining HTML options for the form "Invoice". Where will these options be stored?

A. $$HTMLOptions text field
B. $$HTMLOptions_Invoice text field
C. $$Invoice_HTMLOptions text field
D. HTML Options form event

Question 18

What is the name of the database template used for creating RSS feeds for views in Notes databases?

A. RSS.NTF
B. RSS_Feeds.NTF

C. RSS_Generator.NTF

D. FeedGenerator.NTF

Question 19

What is the purpose of HTML Options included in the design of a form?

A. Disable Passthru HTML

B. Alter the HTML that is generated for the form

C. Alter the HTML that is generated for individual fields on the form

D. All of the above

Question 20

What is the name of the Domino blog template available in Lotus Notes and Domino Release 8?

A. Blog.NTF

B. WebLog.NTF

C. DominoBlog.NTF

D. DominoWebLog.NTF

Question 21

Which of the following can be accomplished by configuring a $$HTMLOptions field on a form?

A. Disable Passthru HTML

B. Force all sections to be expanded

C. Force all outlines to be expanded

D. All of the above

Question 22

Which of the following can be used to open the currently selected document in a new window?

A. @Command([OpenInNewWindow])

B. @OpenDocument([NEWWINDOW])

C. @Command([OpenDocument]; 0)

D. @Command([OpenDocument]; 1)

Question 23

The following statements regarding RSS feed generator databases are true, except:

A. An RSS Feed Generator database must reside on a Domino server
B. An RSS Feed Generator database is based on the RSS_Generator.NTF template
C. An RSS Feed Generator database is used for mapping fields in Notes databases to RSS XML elements
D. An RSS Feed Generator database can access and generate RSS feeds for databases residing on any Domino server within the same domain

Question 24

The KeyType argument of the ReadViewEntries URL command can be set each of the following values except:

A. text
B. date
C. time
D. number

Question 25

What does the term "JIT Compiler" represent related to Java support in Lotus Notes and Domino Release 8?

A. Just In Time Compiler
B. Java Internet Transaction Compiler
C. Java Integrated Technologies Compiler
D. Java Interlaced Threads Compiler

Question 26

What is the purpose of an RSS feed generator database?

A. Map fields in a Notes database to RSS XML elements
B. Generate RSS feeds for a Notes database
C. Syndicate RSS feeds for a Notes database
D. All of the above

Question 27

Which of the following is not a valid HTML Option for a form?

A. DisablePassThruHTML
B. ForceSectionExpand
C. ColumnAtATimeTableAlt
D. RowAtATimeTableAlt

Question 28

Jason is creating a scheduled agent. He would like to use the MarkAllRead method of the NotesView class to mark all documents in a view as read by a specified user. Is this possible?

A. No. The MarkAllRead method cannot be used in a scheduled or background agent.
B. No. The MarkAllRead method would use the server ID as the user name when run from a scheduled or background agent.
C. No. The MarkAllRead method would use the agent signer as the user name when run from a scheduled or background agent.
D. Yes. Include the desired user name as the username parameter in the MarkAllRead method.

Question 29

What will the function @Version return for a scheduled agent running on a Domino Release 8.0 Server?

A. 8
B. 301
C. Notes8
D. Domino8

Question 30

The OutputFormat argument of the ReadViewEntries URL command should be set to which of the following in order to display a view in a JavaScript Object Notation format?

A. JSON
B. Java
C. Script
D. JavaScript

Question 31

What is the purpose of the Subtract method of the NotesViewEntryCollection class?

A. Removes a specified number of documents from the end of the NotesViewEntryCollection
B. Removes a specified number of documents from the beginning of the NotesViewEntryCollection
C. Removes any documents from the NotesViewEntryCollection that exist in the specified secondary collection
D. Creates a NotesDocumentCollection of all documents from the NotesViewEntryCollection that do not exist in the specified secondary collection

Question 32

The following statements regarding the MIMEOption property of the NotesDXLExporter class are true, except:

A. The MIMEOption_DXL option is recommended for exporting mail databases
B. The MIMEOption_RAW option exports the MIME data encoded in Base64
C. The MIMEOption_RAW option (an integer value of 1) is the default for this property
D. The MIMEOption_DXL option was the only DXL format for MIME data prior to Lotus Notes Domino Release 8

Question 33

In Lotus Notes and Domino Release 8, what is the line length limit of a line written by a Write statement in LotusScript?

A. There is no limit
B. 255 Characters
C. 1024 Characters
D. 64K Characters

Question 34

What is the purpose of the Merge method of the NotesViewEntryCollection class?

A. Removes a specified number of documents from the end of the NotesViewEntryCollection
B. Removes a specified number of documents from the beginning of the NotesViewEntryCollection
C. Adds any documents from the NotesViewEntryCollection that exist in the specified secondary collection
D. Creates a NotesDocumentCollection of all documents from the NotesViewEntryCollection that do not exist in the specified secondary collection

Question 35

Which of the following LotusScript file handling routines will remove leading spaces from file name arguments?

A. dir
B. chdir
C. open
D. All of the above

Question 36

Which of the following statements regarding HTML Options is true?

A. Only one HTML option may be defined per field
B. Form-level HTML options override Field-level HTML options
C. Field-level HTML options override Form-level HTML options
D. If Form-level HTML options are defined, Field-level HTML options cannot be used on the form

Question 37

When is the OnSelect event of NotesUIView triggered?

A. When a view is opened in the Notes client
B. When the selected (highlighted) entry is moved from one row in the view to another row
C. When an entry is selected (checked) or deselected (unchecked) in the selection margin of the view
D. All of the above

Question 38

Which of the following best describes the purpose of the JIT Compiler?

A. Compiles JavaScript and LotusScript code into Java bytecode
B. Compiles Java bytecode into JavaScript, HTML, and/or XML, depending on the user's browser type
C. Dynamically compiles Java bytecode to the native platform to optimize performance of Java programs
D. Dynamically creates multiple instances of the Java bytecode for a Java program to run in multiple threads

Question 39

Mary is defining HTML options for the field "Comments". Where will these options be stored?

A. HTML Options form event
B. HTML Options formula of the Comments field
C. $$Comments_HTMLOptions text field
D. $$HTMLOptions_Comments text field

Question 40

What does the acronym URL represent?

A. Universal Resource Library
B. Uniform Resource Locator
C. Unified Response Language
D. Universal Resource Language

Question 41

Which of the following will occur if the size of an HTTP Post request in a Domino database is 65K?

A. The request will fail since the limit for an HTTP Post request in Lotus Notes/Domino is 64K
B. The CGI variable Request_Content will be created with only the first 64K of data from the HTTP Post request. The remainder of data will be lost.
C. The CGI variable Request_Content will be created with only the last 64K of data from the HTTP Post request. The remainder of data will be lost.
D. The CGI variable Request_Content_000 will be created with the first 64K of data from the HTTP Post request and the CGI variable Request_Content_001 will be created with the remaining 1K of data.

Question 42

What does the acronym RSS represent?

A. Remote Server Security
B. Remote Session Security
C. Really Simple Syndication
D. Remote Server Syndication

Question 43

Barbara is creating a LotusScript agent to export documents in the ProductCatalog.nsf database to DXL. She wishes to exclude rich text pictures from the DXL output. Barbara has coded the following:

```
Dim s As New NotesSession
Dim db As NotesDatabase
Dim exp As NotesDXLExporter
Set db = s.CurrentDatabase
Set exp = s.CreateDXLExporter
```

Which of the following should she use to replace each picture in the DXL output with a text message indicating that the picture was removed?

A. Call exp.OmitRichtextPictures(<Picture Removed>)

B. Call exp.OmitRichtextPictures("<Picture Removed>")

C. exp.OmitRichtextPictures = "[Picture Removed]"

D. exp.OmitRichtextPictures = True
   exp.PictureOmittedText = "[Picture Removed]"

Question 44

Which of the following statements regarding the JIT Compiler is true?

A. The JIT Compiler is activated by default
B. The JIT Compiler compiles Java bytecode to the native platform
C. The JIT Compiler compiles dynamically to optimize run time performance of Java programs
D. All of the above

Question 45

Which of the following graphics type elements will be omitted from the DXL output if the OmitRichtextPictures property of the NotesDXLExporter object is set to True?

A. Only items with the \<jpeg\> element
B. Only items with the \<jpeg\> or \<gif\> element
C. Items with the \<jpeg\>, \<gif\>, \<notesbitmap\>, or \<cgm\> elements
D. Items with the \<jpeg\>, \<gif\>, \<bmp\>, \<picture\>, or \<thumbnail\> elements

Question 46

Chris has coded the following to set the value of the "EmployeeType" property.

```
Dim s As New NotesSession
Dim pb As NotesPropertyBroker
Set pb = s.GetPropertyBroker
Call pb.setPropertyValue("EmployeeType","Manager")
```

Which of the following lines of code should he add to ensure that this change will not be lost?

A. Call pb.Save()
B. Call pb.Publish()
C. pb.Publish = True
D. Call pb.Publish("EmployeeType")

Question 47

Sandy has exported documents from the HelpDesk.nsf database to DXL. She used the UncompressAttachments property of NotesDXLExporter to uncompress document attachments in the DXL output. What should she do to ensure that the attachments are not recompressed when importing the documents using the DXL Importer?

A. Remove the desiredcompression attribute from the DXL
B. Set the CompressAttachments property of NotesDXLImporter to True
C. Set the CompressAttachments property of NotesDXLImporter to False
D. Set the UncompressAttachments property of NotesDXLImporter to True

Question 48

Bob would like to populate a NotesDirectoryNavigator with LookupNames matches where the "email" item of the "Contacts" view contains the value "Smith". Partial matches should be allowed. Bob has coded the following:

```
Dim s As New NotesSession
Dim dir As NotesDirectory
Dim nav As NotesDirectoryNavigator
Set dir = s.GetDirectory
```

Which of the following lines of code should he add?

A. Set nav = dir.LookupAllName("Contacts", "Smith", "email")
B. Set nav = dir.LookupNames("Contacts", "Smith", "email", False)
C. Set nav = dir.LookupNames("Contacts", "Smith", "email", True)
D. Set nav = dir.LookupAllName("Contacts", "Smith", "email", True)

Competency Area 5: Web Services in Domino Applications

Question 1

Domino Designer 8 supports which of the following types of Web Services?

A. Consumer Web Services only
B. Provider Web Services only
C. Consumer and Provider Web Services
D. Web Services are not supported in Domino Designer 8

Question 2

Which of the following programming languages can be used to create a consumer Web Service in Domino Designer?

A. HTML and JavaScript
B. LotusScript and Java
C. LotusScript and JavaScript
D. LotusScript, Java, and JavaScript

Question 3

Bill has made some changes to a Web Service in a local copy of the HelpDesk.nsf database. Before moving these changes to production, he would first like to test the Web Service on his local machine. Is this possible?

A. No. The database must reside on a Domino server in order to test a Web Service.
B. Yes. Open the Web Service design element and select the "Run..." action button.
C. Yes. Open the Web Service design element and select "Design > Preview in Default Web Browser" from the menu in the Domino Designer client.
D. Yes. In the Advanced tab of the Web Service Properties, enable the setting "Preview this web service" and choose "Action menu selection" for the trigger. Run the Web Service from the Action menu in the Lotus Notes client.

Question 4

Natalie would like to access a commercially available Web Service from the Notes 8 application he is creating. How could she do this?

A. This cannot be accomplished, because Domino Designer only supports Web Service providers
B. This cannot be accomplished, because Domino Designer only supports Web Service consumers
C. Create a Web Service design element, import the WSDL associated with the Web Service, and create an action or agent to invoke the call to the Web Service
D. Create a Web Service enabled script library, import the WSDL associated with the web service, and create an action or agent to invoke the call to the Web Service

Question 5

What does the acronym WSDL represent?

A. Web Services Description Language
B. Web Services Domino Language
C. Web Security Descriptor Link
D. Web Security Domino Layer

Question 6

How is a LotusScript Web Service-enabled Script Library created in Domino Designer?

A. Select "Shared Code > Web Services" from the Design Pane and click on the "New LotusScript Library" action button
B. Select "Shared Code > LotusScript Libraries" from the Design Pane and click on the "New Web Service" action button
C. Select "Shared Code > Script Libraries" from the Design Pane, click on the "New Web Service" action button, and choose the "LotusScript" language option
D. Select "Shared Code > Script Libraries" from the Design Pane, click on the "New LotusScript Library" action button, and import the WSDL associated with a Web Service

Question 7

Which of the following design elements cannot be previewed locally from Domino Designer?

A. Form
B. View
C. Agent
D. Web Service

Question 8

Which of the following is a true statement regarding Web Services in Lotus Notes and Domino?

A. Both Consumer and Provider Web Services are supported
B. Web Services can be previewed locally from Domino Designer
C. A Web Service can be coded in either LotusScript or Java
D. All of the above

Question 9

How is a web service consumer created in Domino Designer?

A. By creating a web service enabled script library and import the WSDL associated with the web service
B. By creating an Agent design element and choosing the "Web Service" option in the Basics tab of the Agent Properties dialog box
C. By creating an Agent design element and choosing the "Web Service Consumer" option in the Basics tab of the Agent Properties dialog box
D. By creating a Web Service design element and choosing the "Consumer" option in the Basics tab of the Web Service Properties dialog box

Question 10

Jeff created a Web Service in his Notes application. After previewing the Web Service locally, he wishes to stop the Web browser preview without exiting Notes. Is this possible?

A. No. Exiting Notes is the only way to shut down the localhost
B. No. Rebooting the machine is the only way to shut down the localhost
C. Yes. From the main menu, select "File > Tools > Stop Web Service Preview"
D. Yes. From the main menu, select "File > Tools > Stop Local Web Preview Process"

Question 11

Charles created the ProductCatalog LotusScript script library and is enabling it as a web service script library. After selecting the "WSDL > Import WSDL" button and importing the WSDL file for the web service, which of the following will occur?

A. The WSDL file will be converted to LotusScript
B. The WSDL file will be converted to JavaScript
C. The WSDL file will be converted to Java
D. The WSDL file will be converted to DXL

Question 12

Which of the following sub-actions is not available in the "WSDL" action button in a LotusScript script library?

A. Import WSDL
B. Export WSDL
C. Show WSDL
D. Edit WSDL

Question 13

What will happen if you re-import a WSDL file into a Web Service enabled script library after it has been customized?

A. Any customizations to the script library will be overwritten
B. An error message will be displayed and the import process will be aborted

C. The imported WSDL will converted and merged with the existing LotusScript code

D. The imported WSDL will converted and appended to the end of the existing LotusScript code

Question 14

What is the name of the text file that is created in the Notes data directory when a WSDL file in imported into a LotusScript script library?

A. WSDL.XML
B. WSNamespace.XML
C. WSMappings.WSDL
D. WSNamespace.mappings

Question 15

Domino Designer created the text file "WSNamespace.mappings" when a WSDL file was imported into a LotusScript script library. Where will this file be stored?

A. In the user's Notes Data directory
B. In the Notes.ini file of the Domino Server
C. In the WSDL directory of the Domino Server
D. In the WebServices directory of the Domino Server

Chapter 4

Practice Test Answer Key

Competency Area 1: Composite Applications

Question	Answer	Question	Answer
1	D	18	B
2	B	19	A
3	A	20	C
4	C	21	D
5	B	22	A
6	D	23	C
7	C	24	D
8	B	25	A
9	D	26	B
10	C	27	D
11	B	28	C
12	A	29	A
13	D	30	A
14	A	31	B
15	C	32	B
16	D	33	D
17	D	34	C

54

Question	Answer	Question	Answer
35	B	40	C
36	D	41	D
37	D	42	A
38	A	43	C
39	B	44	D

Competency Area 2: Design and Development Enhancements

Question	Answer	Question	Answer
1	B	23	A
2	D	24	C
3	C	25	C
4	B	26	D
5	D	27	D
6	B	28	A
7	C	29	D
8	D	30	A
9	D	31	B
10	B	32	D
11	C	33	A
12	D	34	C
13	B	35	A
14	D	36	D
15	C	37	D
16	B	38	A
17	D	39	D
18	D	40	D
19	C	41	B
20	B	42	A
21	D	43	B
22	B	44	A

Question	**Answer**		**Question**	**Answer**
45	B		49	B
46	D		50	A
47	C		51	D
48	D			

Competency Area 3: Domino and DB2 Integration

Question	Answer	Question	Answer
1	D	8	B
2	B	9	A
3	A	10	A
4	C	11	B
5	C	12	A
6	D	13	D
7	C	14	C

Competency Area 4: Programming Enhancements

Question	Answer		Question	Answer
1	C		23	D
2	B		24	B
3	A		25	A
4	D		26	D
5	C		27	C
6	D		28	D
7	B		29	B
8	C		30	A
9	A		31	C
10	D		32	D
11	B		33	A
12	A		34	C
13	A		35	B
14	C		36	C
15	D		37	D
16	C		38	C
17	A		39	D
18	C		40	B
19	D		41	D
20	C		42	C
21	D		43	D
22	A		44	D

Question	Answer	Question	Answer
45	C	47	A
46	B	48	C

Competency Area 5: Web Services in Domino Applications

Question	Answer		Question	Answer
1	C		9	A
2	B		10	D
3	C		11	A
4	D		12	D
5	A		13	A
6	D		14	D
7	C		15	A
8	D			

Chapter 5

Practice Test Explanations

About the Practice Tests Explanations

The practice test explanations consist of the following information for each of the practice test question items:

- The question
- The correct answer
- The competency area related to the question
- The competency item related to the question
- Topics from the Lotus Notes and Domino Help database(s) related to the question

Competency Area 1: Composite Applications

Question 1

Which type of composite application components are supported in Domino Designer 8?

Correct Answer: D
Eclipse and NSF components

Competency Area: Composite Applications
Competency Item: Understand the advantages and structure of composite applications

Lotus Domino Designer 8 Help Database Topics:
- Elements of composite applications

Question 2

Which client type is used to launch the Composite Application Editor?

Correct Answer: B
Notes 8 Standard Client

Competency Area: Composite Applications
Competency Item: Understand and describe the creation process of a composite application

Lotus Domino Designer 8 Help Database Topics:
- Using the Composite Application Editor

Question 3

What is the name of the managed client software that is used to deploy composite applications hosted on a Domino 8 server?

Correct Answer: A
Lotus Expeditor

Competency Area: Composite Applications
Competency Item: Understand and describe the deployment of a composite application

Lotus Domino Designer 8 Help Database Topics:
- Elements of composite applications

Question 4

What design elements are available in Domino Designer 8 for composite applications?

Correct Answer: C
Wiring Properties and Applications

Competency Area: Composite Applications
Competency Item: Understand and describe the creation process of a composite application

Lotus Domino Designer 8 Help Database Topics:
- Available composite application design elements in Domino Designer

Question 5

The Notes 8 Standard Client is based on which of the following frameworks?

Correct Answer: B
Eclipse

Competency Area: Composite Applications
Competency Item: Understand the advantages and structure of composite applications

Lotus Domino Designer 8 Help Database Topics:
- Setting up your Eclipse environment

Question 6

Which of the following best describes what a composite application is?

Correct Answer: D
An application consisting of a collection of reusable components, from multiple sources, within a service oriented architecture

Competency Area: Composite Applications
Competency Item: Understand and describe the planning process of a composite application

Lotus Domino Designer 8 Help Database Topics:
- Composite applications in IBM Lotus Domino Designer

Question 7

Which composite application design element is used for providing access to WSDL files within a Notes composite application container?

Correct Answer: C
Wiring Properties

Competency Area: Composite Applications
Competency Item: Understand and describe the creation process of a composite application

Lotus Domino Designer 8 Help Database Topics:
- Working with the Wiring Properties design element in Domino Designer

Question 8

Carolyn assembled a composite application using her Lotus Notes 8 client's Composite Application Editor. In order to access this composite application via a Web browser, where can the composite application be hosted?

Correct Answer: B
WebSphere Portal 6 server only

Competency Area: Composite Applications
Competency Item: Understand and describe the deployment of a composite application

Lotus Domino Designer 8 Help Database Topics:
- Elements of composite applications

Question 9

The Composite Application Editor can be used to perform which of the following for composite application components?

Correct Answer: D
All of the above

Competency Area: Composite Applications
Competency Item: Understand and describe the creation process of a composite application

Lotus Domino Designer 8 Help Database Topics:
- Using the Composite Application Editor

Question 10

Which of the following best describes Lotus Expeditor?

Correct Answer: C
A managed client, based on the Eclipse framework, used for deploying composite applications in a service oriented architecture

Competency Area: Composite Applications
Competency Item: Understand and describe the deployment of a composite application

Lotus Domino Designer 8 Help Database Topics:
- Using the Lotus Expeditor Toolkit with Notes as a development environment

Question 11

An application consisting of a collection of reusable components, from multiple sources, within a service oriented architecture is referred to as what?

Correct Answer: B
Composite Application

Competency Area: Composite Applications
Competency Item: Understand and describe the planning process of a composite application

Lotus Domino Designer 8 Help Database Topics:
- Composite applications in IBM Lotus Domino Designer

Question 12

Kelly used the Composite Application Editor to make several changes to the Employee Information composite application hosted on the Domino 8 server CompApps. When will the changes to this composite application take effect?

Correct Answer: A
Immediately

Competency Area: Composite Applications
Competency Item: Understand and describe the creation process of a composite application

Lotus Domino Designer 8 Help Database Topics:
- Using the Composite Application Editor

Question 13

Which of the following tools is used for assembling and wiring composite applications?

Correct Answer: D
Composite Application Editor

Competency Area: Composite Applications
Competency Item: Understand and describe the creation process of a composite application

Lotus Domino Designer 8 Help Database Topics:
- Using the Composite Application Editor

Question 14

Which of the Lotus Notes and Domino Release 8 client products can be installed as either the basic client or the standard Eclipsed-based client?

Correct Answer: A
Lotus Notes client

Competency Area: Composite Applications
Competency Item: Understand and describe the deployment of a composite application

Lotus Domino Designer 8 Help Database Topics:
- About composite applications

Question 15

Which of the following Notes design elements cannot be surfaced as a component in a composite application?

Correct Answer: C
Agent

Competency Area: Composite Applications
Competency Item: Understand and describe the creation process of a composite application

Lotus Domino Designer 8 Help Database Topics:
- Building NSF components

Question 16

The Composite Application Editor can be used to perform which of the following for a composite application?

Correct Answer: D
All of the above

Competency Area: Composite Applications
Competency Item: Understand and describe the creation process of a composite application

Lotus Domino Designer 8 Help Database Topics:
  • Using the Composite Application Editor

Question 17

The Lotus Notes 8 client software can be installed on a workstation with which of the following configurations?

Correct Answer: D
Basic client configuration or Eclipsed-based client configuration

Competency Area: Composite Applications
Competency Item: Understand and describe the deployment of a composite application

Lotus Domino Designer 8 Help Database Topics:
  • About composite applications

Question 18

A design architecture that uses reusable components and loosely coupled services to support business processes is referred to as what?

Correct Answer: B
Service Oriented Architecture (SOA)

Competency Area: Composite Applications
Competency Item: Understand and describe the planning process of a composite application

Lotus Domino Designer 8 Help Database Topics:
  • Composite applications in IBM Lotus Domino Designer

Question 19

Which of the following steps should be performed first when creating a new Notes 8 composite application container using the Notes 8 client?

Correct Answer: A
Select "File > Application > New" and choose the "-Blank Composite Application-" template

Competency Area: Composite Applications
Competency Item: Understand and describe the creation process of a composite application

Lotus Domino Designer 8 Help Database Topics:
- Creating a blank composite application container in the Notes client

Question 20

The Property Broker Editor contains tabs to define each of the following, except:

Correct Answer: C
Schema

Competency Area: Composite Applications
Competency Item: Understand and describe the creation process of a composite application

Lotus Domino Designer 8 Help Database Topics:
- Using the Property Broker Editor feature in Domino Designer

Question 21

Notes 8 composite applications can reside on which of the following?

Correct Answer: D
All of the above

Competency Area: Composite Applications
Competency Item: Understand and describe the deployment of a composite application

Lotus Domino Designer 8 Help Database Topics:
- Elements of composite applications

Question 22

Dale wants to ensure that the elements and attributes in his WSDL files are treated as unique names by the composite applications editor. Which of the following should he do?

Correct Answer: A
Use Namespaces in the WSDL file

Competency Area: Composite Applications
Competency Item: Understand and describe the creation process of a composite application

Lotus Domino Designer 8 Help Database Topics:
- Using the Property Broker Editor feature in Domino Designer

Question 23

Which of the following statements regarding Notes composite application components is false?

Correct Answer: C
Composite applications consisting of Notes components can be hosted on Domino servers running Release 7.02 or later

Competency Area: Composite Applications
Competency Item: Understand and describe the deployment of a composite application

Lotus Domino Designer 8 Help Database Topics:
- Elements of composite applications

Question 24

Which of the following best describes Eclipse?

Correct Answer: D
An open-source framework used for creating integrated development environments and deploying rich client applications

Competency Area: Composite Applications
Competency Item: Understand and describe the planning process of a composite application

Lotus Domino Designer 8 Help Database Topics:
- Setting up your Eclipse environment

Question 25

Where is the composite application wiring panel located?

Correct Answer: A
Composite Application Editor

Competency Area: Composite Applications
Competency Item: Understand and describe the creation process of a composite application

Lotus Domino Designer 8 Help Database Topics:
- Using the Composite Application Editor

Question 26

Which of the following statements regarding the Lotus Notes 8 basic and standard client configurations is false?

Correct Answer: B
Applications accessed from the Lotus Notes 8 standard client must use the optional DB2 data store

Competency Area:	Composite Applications
Competency Item:	Understand and describe the deployment of a composite application

Lotus Domino Designer 8 Help Database Topics:
- About composite applications

Question 27

Which composite application design element is used for providing access to the XML files that contain composite application definitions for a Notes composite application?

Correct Answer: D
Applications

Competency Area:	Composite Applications
Competency Item:	Understand and describe the creation process of a composite application

Lotus Domino Designer 8 Help Database Topics:
- Available composite application design elements in Domino Designer

Question 28

What does the acronym XML represent?

Correct Answer: C
Extensible Markup Language

Competency Area:	Composite Applications
Competency Item:	Understand and describe the deployment of a composite application

Lotus Domino Designer 8 Help Database Topics:
- Using XML with Lotus Domino

Question 29

Design elements of Lotus Notes databases used in a composite applications are known as what?

Correct Answer: A
NSF Components

Competency Area:	Composite Applications
Competency Item:	Understand and describe the creation process of a composite application

Lotus Domino Designer 8 Help Database Topics:
- Elements of composite applications

Question 30

Which of the following best describes the Notes 8 Standard Client architecture?

Correct Answer: A
Notes 8 Standard Client is built on the Lotus Expeditor framework, which is built on the Eclipse framework

Competency Area: Composite Applications
Competency Item: Understand the advantages and structure of composite applications

Lotus Domino Designer 8 Help Database Topics:
- Using the Lotus Expeditor Toolkit with Notes as a development environment

Question 31

What does the acronym SOA represent?

Correct Answer: B
Service Oriented Architecture

Competency Area: Composite Applications
Competency Item: Understand the advantages and structure of composite applications

Lotus Domino Designer 8 Help Database Topics:
- Composite applications in IBM Lotus Domino Designer

Question 32

The "Launch as Composite Application" option in the Launch tab of the Database Properties would work best in which of the following scenarios?

Correct Answer: B
All users of the application will be running the Lotus Notes 8 Standard client

Competency Area: Composite Applications
Competency Item: Understand and describe the deployment of a composite application

Lotus Domino Designer 8 Help Database Topics:
- Creating the composite application

Question 33

Which of the following statements regarding the publishing of properties by NSF components is true?

Correct Answer: D
All of the above

Competency Area: Composite Applications
Competency Item: Understand and describe the creation process of a composite application

Lotus Domino Designer 8 Help Database Topics:
*   Building NSF components

Question 34

Which of the following is a true statement regarding the properties of a composite application component?

Correct Answer: C
A component can consume properties, publish properties, or both

Competency Area: Composite Applications
Competency Item: Understand and describe the planning process of a composite application

Lotus Domino Designer 8 Help Database Topics:
*   A closer look at component interaction

Question 35

Which of the following tools is used for creating and editing the WSDL files for the Composite Application Properties design elements?

Correct Answer: B
Property Broker Editor

Competency Area: Composite Applications
Competency Item: Understand and describe the creation process of a composite application

Lotus Domino Designer 8 Help Database Topics:
*   Using the Property Broker Editor feature in Domino Designer

Question 36

Which of the following can be used to build components for a composite application?

Correct Answer: D
All of the above

Competency Area: Composite Applications
Competency Item: Understand and describe the planning process of a composite application

Lotus Domino Designer 8 Help Database Topics:
- Building your components

Question 37

Which of the follow describes how the Property Broker Editor is launched?

Correct Answer: D
Open a composite application in the Domino Designer 8 client, select a Property design element from the "Composite Applications > Properties" design list, and select the "Open File" action button

Competency Area: Composite Applications
Competency Item: Understand and describe the creation process of a composite application

Lotus Domino Designer 8 Help Database Topics:
- Using the Property Broker Editor feature in Domino Designer

Question 38

Pete has created several composite application components. In order to assemble these components in a composite application for the Lotus Notes 8 client, which of the following best describes the steps to be followed?

Correct Answer: A
First, create a Lotus Notes composite application container. Next, add the components to the composite application container. Finally, wire the components together

Competency Area: Composite Applications
Competency Item: Understand and describe the deployment of a composite application

Lotus Domino Designer 8 Help Database Topics:
- Using the Composite Application Editor

Question 39

Which of the following describes how an NSF component of a composite application can consume a property of another component?

Correct Answer: B
In the Advanced tab of the Action Properties of an action in the Notes design element, select the WSDL action that is wired to receive the property

Competency Area: Composite Applications
Competency Item: Understand and describe the planning process of a composite application

Lotus Domino Designer 8 Help Database Topics:
- Building NSF components

Question 40

Which of the follow describes how the Composite Application Editor is launched?

Correct Answer: C
Open a composite application in the Lotus Notes 8 client and select "Actions > Edit Application"

Competency Area: Composite Applications
Competency Item: Understand and describe the creation process of a composite application

Lotus Domino Designer 8 Help Database Topics:
- Using the Composite Application Editor

Question 41

Pat has created a frameset to open an application as a composite application to the Welcome page. This frameset is specified in the "Open designated Frameset" option in the Launch tab of the Database Properties. What will occur if a user running the Lotus Notes 7 client opens this application?

Correct Answer: D
The Composite Application settings configured in the Frameset Properties will be ignored and the application will open to the designated frameset

Competency Area: Composite Applications
Competency Item: Understand and describe the deployment of a composite application

Lotus Domino Designer 8 Help Database Topics:
Storing the Composite Application in a Notes Database

Question 42

The Property Broker Editor feature of the Domino Designer 8 uses which of the following to define properties, types, and actions?

Correct Answer: A
WSDL

Competency Area: Composite Applications
Competency Item: Understand and describe the creation process of a composite application

Lotus Domino Designer 8 Help Database Topics:
- Using the Property Broker Editor feature in Domino Designer

Question 43

Which of the following will occur when a new composite application container is created from the Notes 8 "-Blank Composite Application-" template?

Correct Answer: C
A page will be displayed in the Notes client indicating that the application does not contain any content

Competency Area: Composite Applications
Competency Item: Understand and describe the creation process of a composite application

Lotus Domino Designer 8 Help Database Topics:
* Creating a blank composite application container in the Notes client

Question 44

Which of the following methods can be used to create a new Notes 8 composite application?

Correct Answer: D
All of the above

Competency Area: Composite Applications
Competency Item: Understand and describe the creation process of a composite application

Lotus Domino Designer 8 Help Database Topics:
* Additional methods for creating Notes-based applications

Competency Area 2: Design and Development Enhancements

Question 1

What is the purpose of the "Show default items in right mouse menu" setting in the Action Bar properties?

Correct Answer: B
Display or hide system default actions in the right-click menu for views and folders

Competency Area: Design and Development Enhancements
Competency Item: Utilize "Show default items in right-mouse menu" option

Lotus Domino Designer 8 Help Database Topics:
- Action bar

Question 2

Which of following statements regarding split button actions is true?

Correct Answer: D
All of the above

Competency Area: Design and Development Enhancements
Competency Item: Utilize "Display as a split button" shared action option

Lotus Domino Designer 8 Help Database Topics:
- Creating and inserting shared actions

Question 3

What is the purpose of the "Extend to use available window width" setting in the Advanced tab of the Column Properties?

Correct Answer: C
Automatically expands any column in the view to fill the width of the viewable window

Competency Area: Design and Development Enhancements
Competency Item: Identify and use advanced options for columns

Lotus Domino Designer 8 Help Database Topics:
- Advanced options for columns

Question 4

If the AnnualSales field contains the value 1,500,000 how will this field be displayed in a view column with the number format of Bytes(K/M/G)?

Correct Answer: B
1.4M

Competency Area: Design and Development Enhancements
Competency Item: Identify and use new view column options

Lotus Domino Designer 8 Help Database Topics:
- Displaying numbers in columns

Question 5

Which of the following view features are available in the Lotus Notes 8 standard client configuration?

Correct Answer: D
All of the above

Competency Area: Design and Development Enhancements
Competency Item: Identify and use advanced options for columns

Lotus Domino Designer 8 Help Database Topics:
- Display options for views

Question 6

Randy added a Rich Text Lite field to a form to include small thumbnail images of screenshots. The Thumbnail option was chosen in the "Limit Input > Only allow" property. However, when a user adds a screenshot image to this field, the image is displayed in its original size. What could Randy do to ensure that these thumbnail images are displayed in a small, uniform size?

Correct Answer: B
Enable the "Resize Thumbnail Image, in pixels" property for the Rich Text Lite field, and enter the desired width and height

Competency Area: Design and Development Enhancements
Competency Item: Utilize new styles of Rich Text Lite fields

Lotus Domino Designer 8 Help Database Topics:
- Text, rich text, and rich text lite fields

Question 7

Eric is creating a new view in a database. Several of the columns in the view have been set up as user-sorted columns. What can Eric do minimize the server performance impact related to the user-sorted columns?

Correct Answer: C
Enable the Column property "Defer index creation until first use" for each user-sorted column in the view

Competency Area: Design and Development Enhancements
Competency Item: Identify and use new view indexing options

Lotus Domino Designer 8 Help Database Topics:
  • Sorting documents in views

Question 8

Kevin is designing a view that includes a column that displays the value of the "Comments" field. He would like to have this column automatically expanded to fill the width of the viewable window. How can he accomplish this?

Correct Answer: D
The Comments column may be any column in the view, and the Column/Advanced property "Extend to use available window width" must be enabled

Competency Area: Design and Development Enhancements
Competency Item: Identify and use advanced options for columns

Lotus Domino Designer 8 Help Database Topics:
  • Advanced options for columns

Question 9

The following statements regarding the "Bytes(K/M/G)" number format in view columns are true, except?

Correct Answer: D
Terabyte values are displayed using scientific notation

Competency Area: Design and Development Enhancements
Competency Item: Identify and use new view column options

Lotus Domino Designer 8 Help Database Topics:
  • Displaying numbers in columns

Question 10

When a view is displayed as a narrow view, how many rows can be displayed for each entry?

Correct Answer: B
Up to two rows per entry will be displayed, depending on the settings in the Column Properties

Competency Area: Design and Development Enhancements
Competency Item: Identify and use advanced options for columns

Lotus Domino Designer 8 Help Database Topics:
- Advanced options for columns

Question 11

Which of the following is not a valid agent event trigger?

Correct Answer: C
When database is opened

Competency Area: Design and Development Enhancements
Competency Item: Manage new agent scheduling options

Lotus Domino Designer 8 Help Database Topics:
- Triggering an agent on an event

Question 12

Which of the following property settings will add information fields to new documents in a database, enabling them to be sorted into a document response hierarchy?

Correct Answer: D
The "Support Response Thread History" setting in the Advanced tab of the Database Properties

Competency Area: Design and Development Enhancements
Competency Item: Identify and use new database property settings

Lotus Domino Designer 8 Help Database Topics:
- Properties that improve database performance

Question 13

Patty is redesigning the "Employee Info" form to display a fixed-sized, thumbnail image of the employee's photo. Which of the following methods bests describes how this can be accomplished?

Correct Answer: B
Create a Rich Text Lite field on the form and open the Control tab of the Field properties. Select "Thumbnail" in the "Only allow" property, enable the "Resize Thumbnail Image in pixels" property and enter the desired width and height in pixels.

Competency Area: Design and Development Enhancements
Competency Item: Utilize new styles of Rich Text Lite fields

Lotus Domino Designer 8 Help Database Topics:
- Text, rich text, and rich text lite fields

Question 14

Users of the Projects.nsf database are indicating that they are unable to use the right-click menu in the Active Projects view to display the Document Properties dialog box for the view entries. What could be causing this behavior?

Correct Answer: D
The Action Bar property "Show default items in right mouse menu" has been disabled

Competency Area: Design and Development Enhancements
Competency Item: Utilize "Show default items in right-mouse menu" option

Lotus Domino Designer 8 Help Database Topics:
- Action bar

Question 15

Robyn, a Domino developer, would like to create a split button action in the Help Desk application. For which client types will the split button feature work?

Correct Answer: C
Notes 8 Standard Client only

Competency Area: Design and Development Enhancements
Competency Item: Utilize "Display as a split button" shared action option

Lotus Domino Designer 8 Help Database Topics:
- Creating and inserting shared actions

Question 16

Which of the following represent all of the valid suffixes that can be displayed in a view column using the "Bytes(K/M/G)" number format?

Correct Answer: B
K, M, G, T

Competency Area: Design and Development Enhancements
Competency Item: Identify and use new view column options

Lotus Domino Designer 8 Help Database Topics:
- Displaying numbers in columns

Question 17

Which of the following best represents the viewers that can be specified in the "Viewers:" setting in the Options tab of the View Properties dialog box?

Correct Answer: D
Table, Tiled, Calendar, and third party viewers

Competency Area:	Design and Development Enhancements
Competency Item:	Identify and use advanced options for columns

Lotus Domino Designer 8 Help Database Topics:
- Display options for views

Question 18

Ron created the BuildProfiles agent in the AppStats.nsf database. He runs this agent manually each time that he restarts the Apps1 server. He would like to automate the execution of this agent. How would he do this?

Correct Answer: D
In the Runtime section of the Agent Properties, select "On event" for the Agent Trigger and select the "When server starts" option

Competency Area:	Design and Development Enhancements
Competency Item:	Manage new agent scheduling options

Lotus Domino Designer 8 Help Database Topics:
- Triggering an agent on an event

Question 19

Which of the following property settings will disable searches from the Search Bar in the Lotus Notes client when a database is not full-text indexed?

Correct Answer: C
Enable the setting "Don't allow simple search" in the Advanced tab of the Database Properties

Competency Area:	Design and Development Enhancements
Competency Item:	Identify and use new database property settings

Lotus Domino Designer 8 Help Database Topics:
- Properties that improve database performance

Question 20

What is the purpose of the Thumbnail option in the Control tab of the Field Properties dialog box?

Correct Answer: B
To display a fixed size image in a Rich Text Lite field

Competency Area: Design and Development Enhancements
Competency Item: Utilize new styles of Rich Text Lite fields

Lotus Domino Designer 8 Help Database Topics:
- Text, rich text, and rich text lite fields

Question 21

What does the acronym ODS represent?

Correct Answer: D
On-Disk Structure

Competency Area: Design and Development Enhancements
Competency Item: Identify and use new database property settings

Lotus Domino Designer 8 Help Database Topics:
- Database Properties box - Info tab

Question 22

If the TotalCalls field contains the value 250, how will this field be displayed in a view column with the number format of Bytes(K/M/G)?

Correct Answer: B
1K

Competency Area: Design and Development Enhancements
Competency Item: Identify and use new view column options

Lotus Domino Designer 8 Help Database Topics:
- Displaying numbers in columns

Question 23

If the BilledHours field contains the value 1,200, how will this field be displayed in a view column with the number format of Bytes(K/M/G)?

Correct Answer: A
1K

Competency Area: Design and Development Enhancements
Competency Item: Identify and use new view column options

Lotus Domino Designer 8 Help Database Topics:
- Displaying numbers in columns

Question 24

Which of following statements regarding split button actions is false?

Correct Answer: C
The icon display settings are disabled in the Action Properties when an action is configured as a split button

Competency Area: Design and Development Enhancements
Competency Item: Utilize "Display as a split button" shared action option

Lotus Domino Designer 8 Help Database Topics:
- Creating and inserting shared actions

Question 25

Which On Disk Structure (ODS) version can a database use in order to take advantage of the Design Note Compression feature?

Correct Answer: C
ODS 48 only

Competency Area: Design and Development Enhancements
Competency Item: Identify and use new database property settings

Lotus Domino 8 Administrator Help Database Topics:
- Allowing database design compression

Question 26

Which of the following features requires the optional On Disk Structure (ODS) version 48?

Correct Answer: D
All of the above

Competency Area: Design and Development Enhancements
Competency Item: Identify and use new database property settings

Lotus Domino 8 Administrator Help Database Topics:
- Allowing database design compression

Question 27

Marcia would like to defer the creation of indexes for user-sorted columns in the views of Projects.nsf database. Where would she go to make this change?

Correct Answer: D
Enable the setting "Defer index creation until first use" in the Sorting tab of the Column Properties dialog box for the user-sorted columns

Competency Area: Design and Development Enhancements
Competency Item: Identify and use new view indexing options

Lotus Domino Designer 8 Help Database Topics:
- Sorting documents in views

Question 28

Which of the following represents the choices available for the Column Properties setting "If view is narrow"?

Correct Answer: A
Keep on top, Hide this column, Wrap to second row

Competency Area: Design and Development Enhancements
Competency Item: Identify and use advanced options for columns

Lotus Domino Designer 8 Help Database Topics:
- Advanced options for columns

Question 29

The Description column is the first column displayed in the Products view. How could the Description column be configured so that it will automatically be expanded to fill the width of the viewable window?

Correct Answer: D
In the Advanced tab of the Column Properties for the Description column, enable the setting "Extend to use available window width"

Competency Area: Design and Development Enhancements
Competency Item: Identify and use advanced options for columns

Lotus Domino Designer 8 Help Database Topics:
- Advanced options for columns

Question 30

What is the purpose of the "Viewers:" setting in the Options tab of the View Properties dialog box?

Correct Answer: A
To specify Table, Tiled, Calendar, and third party viewers that users of composite applications can switch between

Competency Area: Design and Development Enhancements
Competency Item: Identify and use advanced options for columns

Lotus Domino Designer 8 Help Database Topics:
- Display options for views

Question 31

Tara has created several actions in the Projects view that are available in the right-click menu. These are the only actions that users need in the right-click menu for this view. Since the system and default view actions are also displayed in the right-click menu, users must look to the bottom of a long list of menu choices to find the custom view actions. What can Tara do to make these custom view actions more accessible to the users?

Correct Answer: B
In the Action Bar properties, disable the property "Show default items in right mouse menu"

Competency Area: Design and Development Enhancements
Competency Item: Utilize "Show default items in right-mouse menu" option

Lotus Domino Designer 8 Help Database Topics:
- Action bar

Question 32

Which of the following is a characteristic of the Narrow View feature?

Correct Answer: D
All of the above

Competency Area: Design and Development Enhancements
Competency Item: Identify and use advanced options for columns

Lotus Domino Designer 8 Help Database Topics:
- Display options for views

Question 33

Which of the following statements is true, regarding the "Bytes(K/M/G)" number format in view columns?

Correct Answer: A
The values displayed in the column are rounded to the nearest number, but never less than 1K

Competency Area: Design and Development Enhancements
Competency Item: Identify and use new view column options

Lotus Domino Designer 8 Help Database Topics:
- Displaying numbers in columns

Question 34

What is the purpose of the "When server starts" agent trigger option in the Agent Properties?

Correct Answer: C
This is an "On event" trigger that executes the agent each time the Domino server is started

Competency Area: Design and Development Enhancements
Competency Item: Manage new agent scheduling options

Lotus Domino Designer 8 Help Database Topics:
- Triggering an agent on an event

Question 35

Which of the following best describes the purpose of the Notes.ini variable "Designer_ShowPropForJavaViewsUI"?

Correct Answer: A
When enabled on a developer's machine, certain design properties, available only for the Lotus Notes standard client configuration, are displayed in the Domino Designer client.

Competency Area: Design and Development Enhancements
Competency Item: Identify and use advanced options for columns

Lotus Domino Designer 8 Help Database Topics:
- Available composite application design elements in Domino Designer

Question 36

Which of the following statements is true regarding the "Don't allow simple search" setting in the Advanced tab of the Database Properties?

Correct Answer: D
When this setting is enabled, an error message will be displayed if a user attempts to perform a search from the Search Bar in the Lotus Notes client when the database is not full-text indexed

Competency Area: Design and Development Enhancements
Competency Item: Identify and use new database property settings

Lotus Domino Designer 8 Help Database Topics:
- Properties that improve database performance

Question 37

Which of the following is not a valid option in the "Notes using the Eclipse-base UI" section of the Options tab in the View Properties dialog box?

Correct Answer: D
Extend to use available window width

Competency Area: Design and Development Enhancements
Competency Item: Identify and use advanced options for columns

Lotus Domino Designer 8 Help Database Topics:
- View/Folder Properties box - Options tab

Question 38

What is the purpose of the setting "Don't allow simple search" in the Advanced tab of the Database Properties?

Correct Answer: A
To prevent searches against a database that is not full-text indexed

Competency Area: Design and Development Enhancements
Competency Item: Identify and use new database property settings

Lotus Domino Designer 8 Help Database Topics:
- Properties that improve database performance

Question 39

Matt would like to have the second row of the Projects view indented when displayed as a narrow view. Which of the following represents the best way for him to accomplish this?

Correct Answer: D
On the Advanced tab of the Column Properties for a column in the view, choose the setting "If view is narrow: Keep on top" and enable the setting "Justify second row under this column"

Competency Area: Design and Development Enhancements
Competency Item: Identify and use advanced options for columns

Lotus Domino Designer 8 Help Database Topics:
- Advanced options for columns

Question 40

Which of the following statements is true, regarding the Thumbnail option in a Rich Text Lite field?

Correct Answer: D
All of the above

Competency Area: Design and Development Enhancements
Competency Item: Utilize new styles of Rich Text Lite fields

Lotus Domino Designer 8 Help Database Topics:
  • Text, rich text, and rich text lite fields

Question 41

What is the purpose of the "Display as a split button" setting in the Action Properties dialog box?

Correct Answer: B
Allows users to execute the first sub-action action associated with the action button by clicking on the left side of the button or display the list of sub-actions by clicking on the down arrow on the right side of the button

Competency Area: Design and Development Enhancements
Competency Item: Utilize "Display as a split button" shared action option

Lotus Domino Designer 8 Help Database Topics:
  • Creating and inserting shared actions

Question 42

What Notes.ini variable is required in order to make the setting "Display separator above this entry" available in the Outline Entry Properties dialog box?

Correct Answer: A
Designer_ShowPropForJavaViewsUI=1

Competency Area: Design and Development Enhancements
Competency Item: Identify and use advanced options for columns

Lotus Domino Designer 8 Help Database Topics:
  • Available composite application design elements in Domino Designer

Question 43

What is the purpose of the setting "Support Response Thread History" in the Advanced tab of the Database Properties?

Correct Answer: B
Adds information fields to new documents in a database, enabling them to be sorted into a document response hierarchy

Competency Area: Design and Development Enhancements
Competency Item: Identify and use new database property settings

Lotus Domino Designer 8 Help Database Topics:
- Properties that improve database performance

Question 44

Which of the following statements is true, regarding the "Bytes(K/M/G)" number format in view columns?

Correct Answer: A
Kilobytes are displayed with the suffix "K"

Competency Area: Design and Development Enhancements
Competency Item: Identify and use new view column options

Lotus Domino Designer 8 Help Database Topics:
- Displaying numbers in columns

Question 45

Brenda would like to create a split button for an action in the Customers view. However, the setting "Display as a split button" is not being shown in the Action Properties dialog box. What might be causing this?

Correct Answer: B
The Notes.ini variable "Designer_ShowPropForJavaViewsUI" is missing

Competency Area: Design and Development Enhancements
Competency Item: Utilize "Display as a split button" shared action option

Lotus Domino Designer 8 Help Database Topics:
- Available composite application design elements in Domino Designer

Question 46

Which of the following statements is true, regarding the horizontal separator feature for Outlines?

Correct Answer: D
All of the above

Competency Area: Design and Development Enhancements
Competency Item: Identify and use advanced options for columns

Lotus Domino Designer 8 Help Database Topics:
- Selected outline entry properties
- Available composite application design elements in Domino Designer

Question 47

Since the HelpDesk.nsf database is extremely large, Jim would like to prevent searches against the databases. Which of the following would allow him to do this?

Correct Answer: C
In the Advanced tab of the Database Properties, enable the setting "Don't allow simple search"

Competency Area: Design and Development Enhancements
Competency Item: Identify and use new database property settings

Lotus Domino Designer 8 Help Database Topics:
- Properties that improve database performance

Question 48

What is the purpose of the "Defer index creation until first use" setting in the Sorting tab of the Column Properties?

Correct Answer: D
To defer the creation of the sort index for a user-sorted column until a user clicks on the column header to re-sort the view

Competency Area: Design and Development Enhancements
Competency Item: Identify and use new view indexing options

Lotus Domino Designer 8 Help Database Topics:
- Sorting documents in views

Question 49

When a view is displayed as a narrow view, what determines which columns are displayed on the first row and which columns are displayed on the second row?

Correct Answer: B
Multiple columns can be designated as first row columns by choose the setting "If view is narrow: Keep on top" in the Advanced tab of the Column Properties. Columns can be designated as second row columns by choose the setting "If view is narrow: Wrap to second row" in the Advanced tab of the Column Properties.

Competency Area: Design and Development Enhancements
Competency Item: Identify and use advanced options for columns

Lotus Domino Designer 8 Help Database Topics:
- Advanced options for columns

Question 50

Which of the following represents the choices available for the Column Properties setting "For Tile Viewer"?

Correct Answer: A
Display on top, Display on bottom, Hide this column

Competency Area: Design and Development Enhancements
Competency Item: Identify and use advanced options for columns

Lotus Domino Designer 8 Help Database Topics:
- Advanced options for columns

Question 51

Which of the following statements regarding the "Support Response Thread History" setting is true?

Correct Answer: D
All of the above

Competency Area: Design and Development Enhancements
Competency Item: Identify and use new database property settings

Lotus Domino Designer 8 Help Database Topics:
Properties that improve database performance

Competency Area 3: Domino and DB2 Integration

Question 1

What does the acronym DAV represent in a Notes database?

Correct Answer: D
DB2 Access View

Competency Area: Domino and DB2 Integration
Competency Item: Understand and use DB2 Access Views

Lotus Domino Designer 8 Help Database Topics:
- DB2 Access views

Question 2

Which of the following DB2 Access View (DAV) special fields allow developers to create functions that can use information related to the location of the Notes database containing the DAV?

Correct Answer: B
#Server and #Database

Competency Area: Domino and DB2 Integration
Competency Item: Identify and use new DB2 Access View fields

Lotus Domino Designer 8 Help Database Topics:
- Creating a DAV

Question 3

Andy would like to verify that the Notes database he is currently accessing is DB2-enabled. How could he do this?

Correct Answer: A
Look for the message "Database is DB2 Enabled" at the bottom of the Info tab of the Database Properties

Competency Area: Domino and DB2 Integration
Competency Item: Understand and use DB2 Access Views

Lotus Domino Designer 8 Help Database Topics:
- Database Properties box - Info tab

Question 4

Which of the following design elements is a shared resource that enables developers to define DB2 views of data within a DB2-enabled Notes database?

Correct Answer: C
DB2 Access View (DAV)

Competency Area: Domino and DB2 Integration
Competency Item: Understand and use DB2 Access Views

Lotus Domino Designer 8 Help Database Topics:
* DB2 Access views

Question 5

Which of the following DB2 Access View (DAV) special fields allow developers to create DB2 Query Views containing response hierarchies?

Correct Answer: C
#Ref and #RespInfo

Competency Area: Domino and DB2 Integration
Competency Item: Identify and use new DB2 Access View fields

Lotus Domino Designer 8 Help Database Topics:
* Creating a DAV

Question 6

Which of the following statements regarding DB2-enabled Notes databases is true?

Correct Answer: D
All of the above

Competency Area: Domino and DB2 Integration
Competency Item: Understand and use DB2 Access Views

Lotus Domino Designer 8 Help Database Topics:
* DB2 Access views

Question 7

Which of the following statements regarding the naming of a new DB2 Access View (DAV) in Domino Designer is true?

Correct Answer: C
If spaces are entered in the DAV name, they will be converted to underscores when the DAV is saved

Competency Area: Domino and DB2 Integration
Competency Item: Understand and use DB2 Access Views

Lotus Domino Designer 8 Help Database Topics:
- Creating a DAV

Question 8

Gretchen ran the following SQL statement against the DB2 Access View "DAV_ByDept":

```
DELETE from DAV_ByDept where DEPT = 'SALES'
```

This SQL statement failed after processing only 10 of the 25 rows that contained "SALES" in the DEPT column. What will be the impact of running this SQL statement?

Correct Answer: B
Since the operation did not complete successfully, the entire operation is rolled back and no rows will be deleted

Competency Area: Domino and DB2 Integration
Competency Item: Understand and use DB2 Access Views

Lotus Domino Designer 8 Help Database Topics:
- Managing DAVs

Question 9

Colleen created a new DAV design element and notices a yellow triangle icon with an exclamation point beside the DAV name in the DB2 Access Views design list. What does this icon indicate?

Correct Answer: A
An error occurred during the creation of the DAV

Competency Area: Domino and DB2 Integration
Competency Item: Understand and use DB2 Access Views

Lotus Domino Designer 8 Help Database Topics:
- Creating a DAV

Question 10

Which of the following statements regarding SQL transaction processing against DB2 Access Views is true?

Correct Answer: A
Bulk Update transactions are committed as a single transaction. If the operation fails before all rows are updated, the entire transaction is rolled back and no rows will be updated.

Competency Area: Domino and DB2 Integration
Competency Item: Understand and use DB2 Access Views

Lotus Domino Designer 8 Help Database Topics:
- Managing DAVs

Question 11

Dan created a new DB2 Access View (DAV) in the HelpDesk.nsf database. In Domino Designer, he notices a green check mark icon beside the DAV name in the DB2 Access Views design list. What does this icon indicate?

Correct Answer: B
The DAV was successfully created and populated in DB2

Competency Area: Domino and DB2 Integration
Competency Item: Understand and use DB2 Access Views

Lotus Domino Designer 8 Help Database Topics:
- Creating a DAV

Question 12

What does the acronym SQL represent?

Correct Answer: A
Structured Query Language

Competency Area: Domino and DB2 Integration
Competency Item: Understand and use DB2 Query Views

Lotus Domino Designer 8 Help Database Topics:
- DB2 Access views

Question 13

A DB2 Query View can be created to display which of the following?

Correct Answer: D
All of the above

Competency Area: Domino and DB2 Integration
Competency Item: Understand and use DB2 Query Views

Lotus Domino Designer 8 Help Database Topics:
DB2 query views

Question 14

The following statements regarding DB2 Query Views are true, except?

Correct Answer: C
Federated data documents can be opened from a DB2 Query View

Competency Area: Domino and DB2 Integration
Competency Item: Understand and use DB2 Query Views

Lotus Domino Designer 8 Help Database Topics:
DB2 query views

Competency Area 4: Programming Enhancements

Question 1

Which of the following can be used to determine if the @SetViewInfo function was used to filter documents from a view?

Correct Answer: C
@GetViewInfo([IsViewFiltered])

Competency Area: Programming Enhancements
Competency Item: Recognize and use new @Functions as well as new parameters for existing @Functions

Lotus Domino Designer 8 Help Database Topics:
* @GetViewInfo

Question 2

Which of the following can be used to populate a NotesViewEntryCollection with the documents in a view that have been unread by the current user?

Correct Answer: B
The GetAllUnreadEntries method of the NotesView class

Competency Area: Programming Enhancements
Competency Item: Recognize and use new LotusScript classes, properties, and methods

Lotus Domino Designer 8 Help Database Topics:
* GetAllUnreadEntries method

Question 3

Which LotusScript class is used to handle communications between Composite Application components?

Correct Answer: A
NotesPropertyBroker

Competency Area: Programming Enhancements
Competency Item: Recognize and use new LotusScript classes, properties, and methods

Lotus Domino Designer 8 Help Database Topics:
* NotesPropertyBroker class

Question 4

Java support in Notes 8 includes which of the following?

Correct Answer: D
All of the above

Competency Area: Programming Enhancements
Competency Item: Recognize new Java support features

Lotus Domino Designer 8 Help Database Topics:
- Running a Java program

Question 5

Which LotusScript class is used to perform lookups of a Notes directory?

Correct Answer: C
NotesDirectoryNavigator

Competency Area: Programming Enhancements
Competency Item: Recognize and use new LotusScript classes, properties, and methods

Lotus Domino Designer 8 Help Database Topics:
- NotesDirectoryNavigator class

Question 6

Which of the following statements regarding the NotesDirectory class in LotusScript is true?

Correct Answer: D
All of the above

Competency Area: Programming Enhancements
Competency Item: Recognize and use new LotusScript classes, properties, and methods

Lotus Domino Designer 8 Help Database Topics:
- NotesDirectory class

Question 7

The Comments rich text field of a document contains four paragraphs of text with 40 characters in each paragraph. What would the function @AbstractSimple("Comments") return for this document?

Correct Answer: B
A single text string containing the text of the first two paragraphs of the Comments field

Competency Area: Programming Enhancements
Competency Item: Recognize and use new @Functions as well as new parameters for existing @Functions

Lotus Domino Designer 8 Help Database Topics:
- @AbstractSimple

Question 8

Which of the following can be used to create a NotesNoteCollection of all documents in a database that have been read by the current user?

Correct Answer: C
The GetAllReadDocuments method of the NotesDatabase class

Competency Area: Programming Enhancements
Competency Item: Recognize and use new LotusScript classes, properties, and methods

Lotus Domino Designer 8 Help Database Topics:
- GetAllReadDocuments method

Question 9

Which LotusScript class is used for representing a property in a Composite Application?

Correct Answer: A
NotesProperty

Competency Area: Programming Enhancements
Competency Item: Recognize and use new LotusScript classes, properties, and methods

Lotus Domino Designer 8 Help Database Topics:
- NotesProperty class

Question 10

The CalendarFormat @Command can be used to display a calendar view in each of the following formats, except:

Correct Answer: D
One work year

Competency Area: Programming Enhancements
Competency Item: Recognize and use new @Commands as well as new parameters for existing @Commands

Lotus Domino Designer 8 Help Database Topics:
- CalendarFormat @Command

Question 11

Tom is creating a LotusScript agent to export documents in the HelpDesk.nsf database to DXL. He wishes to exclude any rich text field attachments from the DXL output. How can he best accomplish this?

Correct Answer: B
Set the NotesDXLExporter.OmitRichtextAttachments property to True

Competency Area: Programming Enhancements
Competency Item: Recognize and use new LotusScript classes, properties, and methods

Lotus Domino Designer 8 Help Database Topics:
- OmitRichtextAttachments property

Question 12

What does the acronym DXL represent?

Correct Answer: A
Domino XML

Competency Area: Programming Enhancements
Competency Item: Recognize and use new LotusScript classes, properties, and methods

Lotus Domino Designer 8 Help Database Topics:
- Using XML with LotusScript

Question 13

Which of the following can be used to copy selected view entries as a table to the clipboard?

Correct Answer: A
@Command([CopySelectedAsTable])

Competency Area: Programming Enhancements
Competency Item: Recognize and use new @Commands as well as new parameters for existing @Commands

Lotus Domino Designer 8 Help Database Topics:
- CopySelectedAsTable @Command

Question 14

Gene would like to construct a URL that ensures that the last entry returned from a ReadViewEntries URL command is the last entry in a view. Which of the following URL commands should he use?

Correct Answer: C
ReadViewEntries&Endview=1

Competency Area: Programming Enhancements
Competency Item: Recognize and use new web URL commands and parameters

Lotus Domino Designer 8 Help Database Topics:
- URL commands for opening servers, databases, and views

Question 15

Helena would like to construct a URL that will navigate the rows of a view in reverse order. Which of the following URL commands should she use?

Correct Answer: D
ReadViewEntries&NavigateReverse=1

Competency Area: Programming Enhancements
Competency Item: Recognize and use new web URL commands and parameters

Lotus Domino Designer 8 Help Database Topics:
- URL commands for opening servers, databases, and views

Question 16

The following statements regarding the RichTextOption property of the NotesDXLExporter class are true, except:

Correct Answer: C
The RICHTEXTOPTION_RAW option (an integer value of 1) is the default value for this property

Competency Area: Programming Enhancements
Competency Item: Recognize and use new LotusScript classes, properties, and methods

Lotus Domino Designer 8 Help Database Topics:
- RichTextOption property

Question 17

Fran is defining HTML options for the form "Invoice". Where will these options be stored?

Correct Answer: A
$$HTMLOptions text field

Competency Area: Programming Enhancements
Competency Item: Utilize HTML option control at field and form level

Lotus Domino Designer 8 Help Database Topics:
- Controlling the HTML generated for a form

Question 18

What is the name of the database template used for creating RSS feeds for views in Notes databases?

Correct Answer: C
RSS_Generator.NTF

Competency Area: Programming Enhancements
Competency Item: Identify and use new database templates

Lotus Domino Designer 8 Help Database Topics:
- RSS feeds

Question 19

What is the purpose of HTML Options included in the design of a form?

Correct Answer: D
All of the above

Competency Area: Programming Enhancements
Competency Item: Recognize and use new web URL commands and parameters

Lotus Domino Designer 8 Help Database Topics:
- Controlling the HTML generated for a form

Question 20

What is the name of the Domino blog template available in Lotus Notes and Domino Release 8?

Correct Answer: C
DominoBlog.NTF

Competency Area: Programming Enhancements
Competency Item: Identify and use new database templates

Lotus Domino Designer 8 Help Database Topics:
- Domino Web logs (blogs)

Question 21

Which of the following can be accomplished by configuring a $$HTMLOptions field on a form?

Correct Answer: D
All of the above

Competency Area: Programming Enhancements
Competency Item: Utilize HTML option control at field and form level

Lotus Domino Designer 8 Help Database Topics:
  • Controlling the HTML generated for a form

Question 22

Which of the following can be used to open the currently selected document in a new window?

Correct Answer: A
@Command([OpenInNewWindow])

Competency Area: Programming Enhancements
Competency Item: Recognize and use new @Commands as well as new parameters for existing @Commands

Lotus Domino Designer 8 Help Database Topics:
  • OpenInNewWindow @Command

Question 23

The following statements regarding RSS feed generator databases are true, except:

Correct Answer: D
An RSS Feed Generator database can access and generate RSS feeds for databases residing on any Domino server within the same domain

Competency Area: Programming Enhancements
Competency Item: Identify and use new database templates

Lotus Domino Designer 8 Help Database Topics:
  • RSS feeds

Question 24

The KeyType argument of the ReadViewEntries URL command can be set each of the following values except:

Correct Answer: B
date

Competency Area: Programming Enhancements
Competency Item: Recognize and use new web URL commands and parameters

Lotus Domino Designer 8 Help Database Topics:
- URL commands for opening servers, databases, and views

Question 25

What does the term "JIT Compiler" represent related to Java support in Lotus Notes and Domino Release 8?

Correct Answer: A
Just In Time Compiler

Competency Area: Programming Enhancements
Competency Item: Recognize new Java support features

Lotus Domino Designer 8 Help Database Topics:
- Running a Java program

Question 26

What is the purpose of an RSS feed generator database?

Correct Answer: D
All of the above

Competency Area: Programming Enhancements
Competency Item: Identify and use new database templates

Lotus Domino Designer 8 Help Database Topics:
- RSS feeds

Question 27

Which of the following is not a valid HTML Option for a form?

Correct Answer: C
ColumnAtATimeTableAlt

Competency Area: Programming Enhancements
Competency Item: Recognize and use new web URL commands and parameters

Lotus Domino Designer 8 Help Database Topics:
- Controlling the HTML generated for a form

Question 28

Jason is creating a scheduled agent. He would like to use the MarkAllRead method of the NotesView class to mark all documents in a view as read by a specified user. Is this possible?

Correct Answer: D
Yes. Include the desired user name as the username parameter in the MarkAllRead method.

Competency Area: Programming Enhancements
Competency Item: Recognize and use new LotusScript classes, properties, and methods

Lotus Domino Designer 8 Help Database Topics:
- MarkAllRead method

Question 29

What will the function @Version return for a scheduled agent running on a Domino Release 8.0 Server?

Correct Answer: B
301

Competency Area: Programming Enhancements
Competency Item: Recognize and use new @Functions as well as new parameters for existing @Functions

Lotus Domino Designer 8 Help Database Topics:
- @Version

Question 30

The OutputFormat argument of the ReadViewEntries URL command should be set to which of the following in order to display a view in a JavaScript Object Notation format?

Correct Answer: A
JSON

Competency Area: Programming Enhancements
Competency Item: Recognize and use new web URL commands and parameters

Lotus Domino Designer 8 Help Database Topics:
- URL commands for opening servers, databases, and views

Question 31

What is the purpose of the Subtract method of the NotesViewEntryCollection class?

Correct Answer: C
Removes any documents from the NotesViewEntryCollection that exist in the specified secondary collection

Competency Area: Programming Enhancements
Competency Item: Recognize and use new LotusScript classes, properties, and methods

Lotus Domino Designer 8 Help Database Topics:
- Subtract method

Question 32

The following statements regarding the MIMEOption property of the NotesDXLExporter class are true, except:

Correct Answer: D
The MIMEOption_DXL option was the only DXL format for MIME data prior to Lotus Notes Domino Release 8

Competency Area: Programming Enhancements
Competency Item: Recognize and use new LotusScript classes, properties, and methods

Lotus Domino Designer 8 Help Database Topics:
- MIMEOption property

Question 33

In Lotus Notes and Domino Release 8, what is the line length limit of a line written by a Write statement in LotusScript?

Correct Answer: A
There is no limit

Competency Area: Programming Enhancements
Competency Item: Recognize and use new LotusScript language changes

Lotus Domino Designer 8 Help Database Topics:
- Limits on file operations in LotusScript

Question 34

What is the purpose of the Merge method of the NotesViewEntryCollection class?

Correct Answer: C
Adds any documents from the NotesViewEntryCollection that exist in the specified secondary collection

Competency Area: Programming Enhancements
Competency Item: Recognize and use new LotusScript classes, properties, and methods

Lotus Domino Designer 8 Help Database Topics:
- Merge method

Question 35

Which of the following LotusScript file handling routines will remove leading spaces from file name arguments?

Correct Answer: B
chdir

Competency Area: Programming Enhancements
Competency Item: Recognize and use new LotusScript language changes

Lotus Domino Designer 8 Help Database Topics:
- Spaces in LotusScript file names

Question 36

Which of the following statements regarding HTML Options is true?

Correct Answer: C
Field-level HTML options override Form-level HTML options

Competency Area: Programming Enhancements
Competency Item: Recognize and use new web URL commands and parameters

Lotus Domino Designer 8 Help Database Topics:
- Controlling the HTML generated for a form

Question 37

When is the OnSelect event of NotesUIView triggered?

Correct Answer: D
All of the above

Competency Area: Programming Enhancements
Competency Item: Recognize and use new LotusScript classes, properties, and methods

Lotus Domino Designer 8 Help Database Topics:
- OnSelect event

Question 38

Which of the following best describes the purpose of the JIT Compiler?

Correct Answer: C
Dynamically compiles Java bytecode to the native platform to optimize performance of Java programs

Competency Area: Programming Enhancements
Competency Item: Recognize new Java support features

Lotus Domino Designer 8 Help Database Topics:
* Running a Java program

Question 39

Mary is defining HTML options for the field "Comments". Where will these options be stored?

Correct Answer: D
$$HTMLOptions_Comments text field

Competency Area: Programming Enhancements
Competency Item: Utilize HTML option control at field and form level

Lotus Domino Designer 8 Help Database Topics:
* Controlling the HTML generated for a form

Question 40

What does the acronym URL represent?

Correct Answer: B
Uniform Resource Locator

Competency Area: Programming Enhancements
Competency Item: Recognize and use new web URL commands and parameters

Lotus Domino Designer 8 Help Database Topics:
* URL commands for opening servers, databases, and views

Question 41

Which of the following will occur if the size of an HTTP Post request in a Domino database is 65K?

Correct Answer: D
The CGI variable Request_Content_000 will be created with the first 64K of data from the HTTP Post request and the CGI variable Request_Content_001 will be created with the remaining 1K of data.

Competency Area: Programming Enhancements
Competency Item: Recognize and use new LotusScript language changes

Lotus Domino Designer 8 Help Database Topics:
- Table of CGI variable names

Question 42

What does the acronym RSS represent?

Correct Answer: C
Really Simple Syndication

Competency Area: Programming Enhancements
Competency Item: Identify and use new database templates

Lotus Domino Designer 8 Help Database Topics:
- RSS feeds

Question 43

Barbara is creating a LotusScript agent to export documents in the ProductCatalog.nsf database to DXL. She wishes to exclude rich text pictures from the DXL output. Barbara has coded the following:

```
Dim s As New NotesSession
Dim db As NotesDatabase
Dim exp As NotesDXLExporter
Set db = s.CurrentDatabase
Set exp = s.CreateDXLExporter
```

Which of the following should she use to replace each picture in the DXL output with a text message indicating that the picture was removed?

Correct Answer: D
exp.OmitRichtextPictures = True
exp.PictureOmittedText = "[Picture Removed]"

Competency Area: Programming Enhancements
Competency Item: Recognize and use new LotusScript classes, properties, and methods

Lotus Domino Designer 8 Help Database Topics:
- OmitRichtextPictures property
- PictureOmittedText property

Question 44

Which of the following statements regarding the JIT Compiler is true?

Correct Answer: D
All of the above

Competency Area: Programming Enhancements
Competency Item: Recognize new Java support features

Lotus Domino Designer 8 Help Database Topics:
- Running a Java program

Question 45

Which of the following graphics type elements will be omitted from the DXL output if the OmitRichtextPictures property of the NotesDXLExporter object is set to True?

Correct Answer: C
Items with the <jpeg>, <gif>, <notesbitmap>, or <cgm> elements

Competency Area: Programming Enhancements
Competency Item: Recognize and use new LotusScript classes, properties, and methods

Lotus Domino Designer 8 Help Database Topics:
- OmitRichtextPictures property

Question 46

Chris has coded the following to set the value of the "EmployeeType" property.

```
Dim s As New NotesSession
Dim pb As NotesPropertyBroker
Set pb = s.GetPropertyBroker
Call pb.setPropertyValue("EmployeeType","Manager")
```

Which of the following lines of code should he add to ensure that this change will not be lost?

Correct Answer: B
Call pb.Publish()

Competency Area: Programming Enhancements
Competency Item: Recognize and use new LotusScript classes, properties, and methods

Lotus Domino Designer 8 Help Database Topics:
- Publish method

Question 47

Sandy has exported documents from the HelpDesk.nsf database to DXL. She used the UncompressAttachments property of NotesDXLExporter to uncompress document attachments in the DXL output. What should she do to ensure that the attachments are not recompressed when importing the documents using the DXL Importer?

Correct Answer: A
Remove the desiredcompression attribute from the DXL

Competency Area: Programming Enhancements
Competency Item: Recognize and use new LotusScript classes, properties, and methods

Lotus Domino Designer 8 Help Database Topics:
- UncompressAttachments property

Question 48

Bob would like to populate a NotesDirectoryNavigator with LookupNames matches where the "email" item of the "Contacts" view contains the value "Smith". Partial matches should be allowed. Bob has coded the following:

```
Dim s As New NotesSession
Dim dir As NotesDirectory
Dim nav As NotesDirectoryNavigator
Set dir = s.GetDirectory
```

Which of the following lines of code should he add?

Correct Answer: C
Set nav = dir.LookupNames("Contacts", "Smith", "email", True)

Competency Area: Programming Enhancements
Competency Item: Recognize and use new LotusScript classes, properties, and methods

Lotus Domino Designer 8 Help Database Topics:
- LookupNames method

Competency Area 5: Web Services in Domino Applications

Question 1

Domino Designer 8 supports which of the following types of Web Services?

Correct Answer: C
Consumer and Provider Web Services

Competency Area: Web Services in Domino Applications
Competency Item: Create a Web Service Consumer

Lotus Domino Designer 8 Help Database Topics:
- Creating web service consumers

Question 2

Which of the following programming languages can be used to create a consumer Web Service in Domino Designer?

Correct Answer: B
LotusScript and Java

Competency Area: Web Services in Domino Applications
Competency Item: Create a Web Service Consumer

Lotus Domino Designer 8 Help Database Topics:
- Creating web service consumers

Question 3

Bill has made some changes to a Web Service in a local copy of the HelpDesk.nsf database. Before moving these changes to production, he would first like to test the Web Service on his local machine. Is this possible?

Correct Answer: C
Yes. Open the Web Service design element and select "Design > Preview in Default Web Browser" from the menu in the Domino Designer client.

Competency Area: Web Services in Domino Applications
Competency Item: Understand and utilize local preview of Web Services

Lotus Domino Designer 8 Help Database Topics:
- Previewing Web services

Question 4

Natalie would like to access a commercially available Web Service from the Notes 8 application he is creating. How could she do this?

Correct Answer: D
Create a Web Service enabled script library, import the WSDL associated with the web service, and create an action or agent to invoke the call to the Web Service

Competency Area: Web Services in Domino Applications
Competency Item: Create a Web Service Consumer

Lotus Domino Designer 8 Help Database Topics:
*   Creating web service consumers

Question 5

What does the acronym WSDL represent?

Correct Answer: A
Web Services Description Language

Competency Area: Web Services in Domino Applications
Competency Item: Create a Web Service Consumer

Lotus Domino Designer 8 Help Database Topics:
*   Web services

Question 6

How is a LotusScript Web Service-enabled Script Library created in Domino Designer?

Correct Answer: D
Select "Shared Code > Script Libraries" from the Design Pane, click on the "New LotusScript Library" action button, and import the WSDL associated with a Web Service

Competency Area: Web Services in Domino Applications
Competency Item: Create a Web Service Consumer

Lotus Domino Designer 8 Help Database Topics:
*   Creating web service consumers

Question 7

Which of the following design elements cannot be previewed locally from Domino Designer?

Correct Answer: C
Agent

Competency Area: Web Services in Domino Applications
Competency Item: Understand and utilize local preview of Web Services

Lotus Domino Designer 8 Help Database Topics:
- Previewing Web services

Question 8

Which of the following is a true statement regarding Web Services in Lotus Notes and Domino?

Correct Answer: D
All of the above

Competency Area: Web Services in Domino Applications
Competency Item: Understand and utilize local preview of Web Services

Lotus Domino Designer 8 Help Database Topics:
- Previewing Web services
- Creating web service consumers

Question 9

How is a web service consumer created in Domino Designer?

Correct Answer: A
By creating a web service enabled script library and import the WSDL associated with the web service

Competency Area: Web Services in Domino Applications
Competency Item: Create a Web Service Consumer

Lotus Domino Designer 8 Help Database Topics:
- Creating web service consumers

Question 10

Jeff created a Web Service in his Notes application. After previewing the Web Service locally, he wishes to stop the Web browser preview without exiting Notes. Is this possible?

Correct Answer: D
Yes. From the main menu, select "File > Tools > Stop Local Web Preview Process"

Competency Area: Web Services in Domino Applications
Competency Item: Understand and utilize local preview of Web Services

Lotus Domino Designer 8 Help Database Topics:
- Previewing Web services

Question 11

Charles created the ProductCatalog LotusScript script library and is enabling it as a web service script library. After selecting the "WSDL > Import WSDL" button and importing the WSDL file for the web service, which of the following will occur?

Correct Answer: A
The WSDL file will be converted to LotusScript

Competency Area: Web Services in Domino Applications
Competency Item: Create a Web Service Consumer

Lotus Domino Designer 8 Help Database Topics:
- Creating web service consumers

Question 12

Which of the following sub-actions is not available in the "WSDL" action button in a LotusScript script library?

Correct Answer: D
Edit WSDL

Competency Area: Web Services in Domino Applications
Competency Item: Create a Web Service Consumer

Lotus Domino Designer 8 Help Database Topics:
- Creating web service consumers

Question 13

What will happen if you re-import a WSDL file into a Web Service enabled script library after it has been customized?

Correct Answer: A
Any customizations to the script library will be overwritten

Competency Area: Web Services in Domino Applications
Competency Item: Create a Web Service Consumer

Lotus Domino Designer 8 Help Database Topics:
- Creating web service consumers

Question 14

What is the name of the text file that is created in the Notes data directory when a WSDL file in imported into a LotusScript script library?

Correct Answer: D
WSNamespace.mappings

Competency Area: Web Services in Domino Applications
Competency Item: Create a Web Service Consumer

Lotus Domino Designer 8 Help Database Topics:
- Creating web service consumers

Question 15

Domino Designer created the text file "WSNamespace.mappings" when a WSDL file was imported into a LotusScript script library. Where will this file be stored?

Correct Answer: A
In the user's Notes Data directory

Competency Area: Web Services in Domino Applications
Competency Item: Create a Web Service Consumer

Lotus Domino Designer 8 Help Database Topics:
- Creating web service consumers

Chapter 6

Flash Cards

About the Flash Cards

The flash card items can be used to help you memorize key concepts and information related to the exam competencies. Each flash card item has the question printed on the front side of the card with the corresponding answer printed on the reverse side. You might want to remove the flash card pages from the book, separate them, and carry them around to review them whenever you have a free moment.

Competency Area 1: Composite Applications

Item 1	Item 2
In Notes 8, an application consisting of a collection of reusable components, from multiple sources, within a service oriented architecture is referred to as what?	A design architecture that uses reusable components and loosely coupled services to support business processes is referred to as what?
Item 3	**Item 4**
Where is the composite application wiring panel located?	What are the two types of composite application components supported in Domino Designer 8?

Item 2
A design architecture that uses reusable components and loosely coupled services to support business processes is referred to as what?

Service Oriented Architecture (SOA)

Item 1
In Notes 8, an application consisting of a collection of reusable components, from multiple sources, within a service oriented architecture is referred to as what?

Composite Application

Item 4
What are the two types of composite application components supported in Domino Designer 8?

Eclipse and NSF components

Item 3
Where is the composite application wiring panel located?

In the Composite Application Editor

Item 5

Which client type is used to launch the Composite Application Editor?

Item 6

What two design elements are available in Domino Designer 8 for creating composite applications?

Item 7

What is the name of the tool in Notes and Domino 8 that is used for assembling and wiring composite applications?

Item 8

Design elements of a Lotus Notes database that are surfaced in a composite applications are known as what?

Item 9

In order to access a Notes 8 composite application via a Web browser, where can the composite application be hosted? A Domino 8 server, a WebSphere Portal server, or either?

Item 10

What is the name of the managed client, based on the Eclipse framework, used for deploying Notes 8 composite applications in a service oriented architecture?

Item 11

How is the Composite Application Editor launched for a Notes 8 composite application?

Item 12

What Domino Designer tool is used for creating and editing the WSDL files for the Composite Application Properties design elements?

Item 6
What two design elements are available in Domino Designer 8 for creating composite applications?

Wiring Properties and Applications

Item 5
Which client type is used to launch the Composite Application Editor?

Notes 8 Standard Client

Item 8
Design elements of a Lotus Notes database that are surfaced in a composite applications are known as what?

NSF Components

Item 7
What is the name of the tool in Notes and Domino 8 that is used for assembling and wiring composite applications?

Composite Application Editor (CAE)

Item 10
What is the name of the managed client, based on the Eclipse framework, used for deploying Notes 8 composite applications in a service oriented architecture?

Lotus Expeditor

Item 9
In order to access a Notes 8 composite application via a Web browser, where can the composite application be hosted? A Domino 8 server, a WebSphere Portal server, or either?

A WebSphere Portal server

Item 12
What Domino Designer tool is used for creating and editing the WSDL files for the Composite Application Properties design elements?

Property Broker Editor (PBE)

Item 11
How is the Composite Application Editor launched for a Notes 8 composite application?

By selecting "Actions > Edit Application" from the main menu of the Lotus Notes 8 Standard client

Item 13

What will happen when a Wiring Property design element is selected from the "Composite Applications > Properties" design list, and the "Open File" action button is clicked?

Item 14

What type of application can include Lotus Notes NSF components, Eclipse components, and Lotus Component Designer components in a single user application?

Item 15

What development environment is used to build NSF components for a Notes 8 composite application?

Item 16

What development environment is used to build Eclipse components for a composite application?

Item 17

A composite application component can have what impact on the properties of a component? Consume properties, publish properties, or both?

Item 18

What two methods can be used for a composite application component to publish a property?

Item 19

Which composite application design element is used for providing access to WSDL files within a Notes composite application container?

Item 20

Which composite application design element is used for providing access to the XML files that contain composite application definitions for a Notes composite application?

Item 14

What type of application can include Lotus Notes NSF components, Eclipse components, and Lotus Component Designer components in a single user application?

Composite Application

Item 13

What will happen when a Wiring Property design element is selected from the "Composite Applications > Properties" design list, and the "Open File" action button is clicked?

The Property Broker Editor will be launched

Item 16

What development environment is used to build Eclipse components for a composite application?

An Eclipse IDE or Rational Application Developer (RAD)

Item 15

What development environment is used to build NSF components for a Notes 8 composite application?

Domino Designer

Item 18

What two methods can be used for a composite application component to publish a property?

[1] Use the LotusScript API; [2] Associate a view/folder column to an output property defined in the WSDL file

---

Item 17

A composite application component can have what impact on the properties of a component? Consume properties, publish properties, or both?

Both

Item 20

Which composite application design element is used for providing access to the XML files that contain composite application definitions for a Notes composite application?

Applications

Item 19

Which composite application design element is used for providing access to WSDL files within a Notes composite application container?

Wiring Properties

Item 21

If changes are made to a Notes 8 composite application using the Composite Application Editor, when will the changes take effect for users accessing the application?

Item 22

What can be used in the WSDL code to ensure that the elements and attributes of a WSDL files are treated as unique names by the composite applications editor?

Item 23

Which Lotus Notes and Domino Release 8 client products can be installed as either the basic client or the standard Eclipsed-based client? The Lotus Notes client, the Domino Designer client, or both?

Item 24

What is the name of the framework that the Lotus Notes 8 Standard client is built on?

Item 25

What does the acronym SOA represent?

Item 26

How is a new Notes 8 composite application container created using the Notes 8 client?

Item 27

On which three platforms can a Notes 8 composite application reside?

Item 28

Which design template should be chosen in order to create a new Notes 8 composite application container?

Item 22
What can be used in the WSDL code to ensure that the elements and attributes of a WSDL files are treated as unique names by the composite applications editor?

Use Namespaces

Item 21
If changes are made to a Notes 8 composite application using the Composite Application Editor, when will the changes take effect for users accessing the application?

Immediately

Item 24
What is the name of the framework that the Lotus Notes 8 Standard client is built on?

Eclipse framework

Item 23
Which Lotus Notes and Domino Release 8 client products can be installed as either the basic client or the standard Eclipsed-based client? The Lotus Notes client, the Domino Designer client, or both?

Lotus Notes client

Item 26
How is a new Notes 8 composite application container created using the Notes 8 client?

Select "File > Application > New" and choose the "-Blank Composite Application-" template

Item 25
What does the acronym SOA represent?

Service Oriented Architecture

Item 28
Which design template should be chosen in order to create a new Notes 8 composite application container?

The "-Blank Composite Application-" template

Item 27
On which three platforms can a Notes 8 composite application reside?

Domino 8 Server, WebSphere Portal 6 Server, and a local machine running the Lotus Notes 8 Client

Item 29

What message is displayed in the Notes Client when a new composite application container is created from the Notes 8 "-Blank Composite Application-" template?

Item 30

The Property Broker Editor feature of the Domino Designer 8 uses which language to define properties, types, and actions?

Item 31

Which Notes design elements can be surfaced as NSF components in composite application?

Item 32

To use the Lotus Notes console for troubleshooting the component loading process for a composite application, what argument should be added to the startup command for the Lotus Notes application shortcut?

Item 30

The Property Broker Editor feature of the Domino Designer 8 uses which language to define properties, types, and actions?

WSDL

Item 29

What message is displayed in the Notes Client when a new composite application container is created from the Notes 8 "-Blank Composite Application-" template?

The message "This application page does not contain any content" is displayed

Item 32

To use the Lotus Notes console for troubleshooting the component loading process for a composite application, what argument should be added to the startup command for the Lotus Notes application shortcut?

-console

Item 31

Which Notes design elements can be surfaced as NSF components in composite application?

Pages, Forms, Views, Folders, Frameset, Navigators

Competency Area 2: Design and Development Enhancements

Item 1 Which field types support the Thumbnail object type?	**Item 2** How can a developer prevent the default system actions from displaying in the right-click context menu of a view?
Item 3 What determines which suffix is displayed if a view column uses the "Bytes(K/M/G)" number format?	**Item 4** What are the suffixes that will be displayed if a view column uses the "Bytes(K/M/G)" number format?
Item 5 In a view column using the "Bytes(K/M/G)" number format, how many Bytes does a Kilobyte (K) represent?	**Item 6** In a view column using the "Bytes(K/M/G)" number format, how many Bytes does a Megabyte (M) represent?
Item 7 In a view column using the "Bytes(K/M/G)" number format, how many Bytes does a Gigabyte (G) represent?	**Item 8** In a view column using the "Bytes(K/M/G)" number format, how many Bytes does a Terabyte (T) represent?

Item 2

How can a developer prevent the default system actions from displaying in the right-click context menu of a view?

Disable the Action Bar Properties setting "Show default items in right mouse menu"

Item 1

Which field types support the Thumbnail object type?

Only the "Rich Text Lite" field type

Item 4

What are the suffixes that will be displayed if a view column uses the "Bytes(K/M/G)" number format?

K, M, G, and T (for Kilobytes. Megabytes, Gigabytes, and Terabytes)

Item 3

What determines which suffix is displayed if a view column uses the "Bytes(K/M/G)" number format?

The size of the number

Item 6

In a view column using the "Bytes(K/M/G)" number format, how many Bytes does a Megabyte (M) represent?

1,048,576 Bytes (1024 Kilobytes)

Item 5

In a view column using the "Bytes(K/M/G)" number format, how many Bytes does a Kilobyte (K) represent?

1024 Bytes

Item 8

In a view column using the "Bytes(K/M/G)" number format, how many Bytes does a Terabyte (T) represent?

1,099,511,627,776 Bytes (1024 Gigabytes)

Item 7

In a view column using the "Bytes(K/M/G)" number format, how many Bytes does a Gigabyte (G) represent?

1,073,741,824 Bytes (1024 Megabytes)

Item 9

Which object type can be selected in the "Limit Input" section of the Field Properties of a Rich Text Lite field to display a fixed-sized image on a form?

Item 10

What is the purpose of the Action Bar Properties setting "Show default items in right mouse menu"?

Item 11

If a view column uses the "Bytes(K/M/G)" number format, are numbers rounded or truncated?

Item 12

What is the minimum value that will be displayed in a view column using the "Bytes(K/M/G)" number format?

Item 13

If multiple object types are selected in the "Limit Input" section of the Field Properties of a Rich Text Lite field, what will happen if the Thumbnail option is selected?

Item 14

If the Thumbnail option is selected in the "Limit Input" section of the Field Properties of a Rich Text Lite field, what will happen if any other option is selected for this setting?

Item 15

What does the acronym ODS represent?

Item 16

What setting in Column Properties can be enabled to help minimize the server performance impact related to the creation of indices for user-sorted columns?

Item 10

What is the purpose of the Action Bar Properties setting "Show default items in right mouse menu"?

Displays or hides system actions in right-click context menu of a view or folder

Item 9

Which object type can be selected in the "Limit Input" section of the Field Properties of a Rich Text Lite field to display a fixed-sized image on a form?

Thumbnail

Item 12

What is the minimum value that will be displayed in a view column using the "Bytes(K/M/G)" number format?

1K

Item 11

If a view column uses the "Bytes(K/M/G)" number format, are numbers rounded or truncated?

Rounded (but never less than 1K)

Item 14

If the Thumbnail option is selected in the "Limit Input" section of the Field Properties of a Rich Text Lite field, what will happen if any other option is selected for this setting?

The Thumbnail option is automatically deselected

Item 13

If multiple object types are selected in the "Limit Input" section of the Field Properties of a Rich Text Lite field, what will happen if the Thumbnail option is selected?

All other options are automatically deselected

Item 16

What setting in Column Properties can be enabled to help minimize the server performance impact related to the creation of indices for user-sorted columns?

The setting "Defer index creation until first use"

Item 15

What does the acronym ODS represent?

On-Disk Structure

Item 17

How many decimal places are displayed for numbers if a view column uses the "Bytes(K/M/G)" number format?

Item 18

What setting in a Rich Text Lite field will ensure that thumbnail images are displayed in a fixed size?

Item 19

What is the optional On Disk Structure (ODS) version number for Notes 8 databases?

Item 20

What is the default On Disk Structure (ODS) version number for Notes 8 databases?

Item 21

What Notes.ini variable must be present in the Notes.ini file in order for a developer to create a Split Button Action?

Item 22

If an agent should only run when a Domino Server starts, which settings in the Runtime section of the Agent Properties should be selected?

Item 23

What setting, when enabled in the Advanced tab of the Database Properties, will add information fields to new documents in a database, allowing them to be sorted into a document response hierarchy?

Item 24

What setting, when enabled in the Advanced tab of the Database Properties, will disable searches from the Search Bar in the Lotus Notes client when a database is not full-text indexed?

Item 18
What setting in a Rich Text Lite field will ensure that thumbnail images are displayed in a fixed size?

The "Resize Thumbnail Image, in pixels" setting

Item 17
How many decimal places are displayed for numbers if a view column uses the "Bytes(K/M/G)" number format.?

One decimal place for Megabytes (M), Gigabytes (G), and Terabytes (T). Kilobytes (K) display whole numbers only.

Item 20
What is the default On Disk Structure (ODS) version number for Notes 8 databases?

ODS 43 (the same as Notes 7 databases)

Item 19
What is the optional On Disk Structure (ODS) version number for Notes 8 databases?

ODS 48

Item 22
If an agent should only run when a Domino Server starts, which settings in the Runtime section of the Agent Properties should be selected?

Select "On event" for the agent trigger and "When server starts" for the option

Item 21
What Notes.ini variable must be present in the Notes.ini file in order for a developer to create a Split Button Action?

Designer_ShowPropForJavaViewsUI=1

Item 24
What setting, when enabled in the Advanced tab of the Database Properties, will disable searches from the Search Bar in the Lotus Notes client when a database is not full-text indexed?

The "Don't allow simple search" setting

Item 23
What setting, when enabled in the Advanced tab of the Database Properties, will add information fields to new documents in a database, allowing them to be sorted into a document response hierarchy?

The "Support Response Thread History" setting

Item 25

If a view in a Notes 8 database is being displayed as a Narrow View, what type of orientation will this view have? Vertical or horizontal?

Item 26

What setting must be enabled in the Advanced tab of the Column Properties for a column, in order to indent the second row when the view is being displayed as a Narrow View?

Item 27

In order to use the Design Note Compression for a Notes 8 database, which On Disk Structure (ODS) must the database use?

Item 28

What Notes.ini variable is used for creating new databases with On Disk Structure (ODS) version 48?

Item 29

What are the three choices available for the Column Properties setting "If view is narrow"?

Item 30

When a view is displayed as a narrow view, what settings in the Advanced tab of the Column Properties will determine which columns are displayed on the first row and which columns are displayed on the second row?

Item 31

When a view is displayed as a narrow view, how many rows can be displayed for each entry?

Item 32

What viewer types can be specified in the "Viewers:" setting in the Options tab of the View Properties dialog box?

Item 26

What setting must be enabled in the Advanced tab of the Column Properties for a column, in order to indent the second row when the view is being displayed as a Narrow View?

The setting "Justify second row under this column"

Item 25

If a view in a Notes 8 database is being displayed as a Narrow View, what type of orientation will this view have? Vertical or horizontal?

Vertical orientation

Item 28

What Notes.ini variable is used for creating new databases with On Disk Structure (ODS) version 48?

Create_R8_Databases=1

Item 27

In order to use the Design Note Compression for a Notes 8 database, which On Disk Structure (ODS) must the database use?

ODS 48

Item 30

When a view is displayed as a narrow view, what settings in the Advanced tab of the Column Properties will determine which columns are displayed on the first row and which columns are displayed on the second row?

The "If view is narrow:" setting "Keep on top" will display a column on the first row. The "If view is narrow:" setting "Wrap to second row" will display a column on the second row if wrapping is necessary.

Item 29

What are the three choices available for the Column Properties setting "If view is narrow"?

Keep on top, Hide this column, Wrap to second row

Item 32

What viewer types can be specified in the "Viewers:" setting in the Options tab of the View Properties dialog box?

Table, Tiled, Calendar, and third party viewers

Item 31

When a view is displayed as a narrow view, how many rows can be displayed for each entry?

Up to two rows per entry

Item 33

What is the purpose of the setting "Don't allow simple search" in the Advanced tab of the Database Properties?

Item 34

What setting, when enabled in the Sorting tab of the Column Properties of a user-sorted column, will defer the creation of the sort index for that column until a user clicks on the column header to re-sort the view?

Item 35

What will happen when a user clicks on the left side of a split button action?

Item 36

What will happen when a user clicks on the down arrow on the right side of a split button action?

Item 37

If the setting "Don't allow simple search" is enabled in the Advanced tab of the Database Properties, what will happen if a user attempts to perform a search from the Search Bar in the Lotus Notes client when the database is not full-text indexed?

Item 38

The "Display as a split button" setting in the Action Properties dialog box can be enabled for which type of action? A parent action, a sub-action, or both?

Item 39

A split button action can be created for which type of design element(s)?

Item 40

The split button feature for actions will work for which client types?

Item 34

What setting, when enabled in the Sorting tab of the Column Properties of a user-sorted column, will defer the creation of the sort index for that column until a user clicks on the column header to re-sort the view?

The "Defer index creation until first use" setting

Item 33

What is the purpose of the setting "Don't allow simple search" in the Advanced tab of the Database Properties?

To prevent searches against a database that is not full-text indexed

Item 36

What will happen when a user clicks on the down arrow on the right side of a split button action?

A list of sub-actions associated with that split button action will be displayed as a drop-down menu

Item 35

What will happen when a user clicks on the left side of a split button action?

The first sub-action associated with that split button action will be executed

Item 38

The "Display as a split button" setting in the Action Properties dialog box can be enabled for which type of action? A parent action, a sub-action, or both?

Only a parent action, with one or more sub-actions, can be enabled as a split button

Item 37

If the setting "Don't allow simple search" is enabled in the Advanced tab of the Database Properties, what will happen if a user attempts to perform a search from the Search Bar in the Lotus Notes client when the database is not full-text indexed?

The error message "Application must be full text indexed before search is allowed" will be displayed

Item 40

The split button feature for actions will work for which client types?

Notes 8 Standard Client only

Item 39

A split button action can be created for which type of design element(s)?

Views and Folders

Item 41

How can a view column, which is not the last column in the view, be configured so that it will automatically be expanded to fill the width of the viewable window?

Item 42

In order to create a split button action in a Notes 8 database, what Notes.ini variable must be included on the machine running the Domino Designer client?

Item 43

Horizontal separators created between entries in an outline design element can be seen by users running which Notes 8 client type? Notes 8 Standard client, Notes 8 Basic client, or both?

Item 44

What Notes.ini variable must be included on a Domino 8 Server to allow a Notes 8 database to defer the creation of indices for user-sorted columns?

Item 45

What choices are available for the Column Properties setting "For Tile Viewer"?

Item 46

Which option, when enabled in the Info Tab of the View Properties, displays icons in the action bar of the view that allows users to switch between horizontal and vertical orientations?

Item 47

What field is added to documents in a database when the setting "Support Response Thread History" is enabled in the Advanced tab of the Database Properties?

Item 48

What documents in a database will have new information fields added when the setting "Support Response Thread History" is enabled in the Advanced tab of the Database Properties? Existing documents, new documents, or all documents in the database?

Item 42

In order to create a split button action in a Notes 8 database, what Notes.ini variable must be included on the machine running the Domino Designer client?

Designer_ShowPropForJavaViewsUI = 1

Item 41

How can a view column, which is not the last column in the view, be configured so that it will automatically be expanded to fill the width of the viewable window?

Enable the setting "Extend to use available window width" in the Advanced tab of the Column Properties for the column.

Item 44

What Notes.ini variable must be included on a Domino 8 Server to allow a Notes 8 database to defer the creation of indices for user-sorted columns?

ENABLE_ON_DEMAND_COLLATIONS=1

Item 43

Horizontal separators created between entries in an outline design element can be seen by users running which Notes 8 client type? Notes 8 Standard client, Notes 8 Basic client, or both?

Notes 8 Standard client

Item 46

Which option, when enabled in the Info Tab of the View Properties, displays icons in the action bar of the view that allows users to switch between horizontal and vertical orientations?

Show Vertical/Horizontal switcher

Item 45

What choices are available for the Column Properties setting "For Tile Viewer"?

Display on top, Display on bottom, Hide this column

Item 48

What documents in a database will have new information fields added when the setting "Support Response Thread History" is enabled in the Advanced tab of the Database Properties? Existing documents, new documents, or all documents in the database?

Only new documents

Item 47

What field is added to documents in a database when the setting "Support Response Thread History" is enabled in the Advanced tab of the Database Properties?

$TUA

Competency Area 3: Domino and DB2 Integration

Item 1 What are the special DAV fields that provide metadata about the Notes database containing the DAV?	**Item 2** What does the acronym DAV represent in a Notes database?
Item 3 What does a DB2 Query View use for selection criteria?	**Item 4** What does the acronym SQL represent?
Item 5 What two special DAV metadata fields allow developers to create functions that can use information related to the location of the Notes database containing the DAV?	**Item 6** What two special DAV metadata fields allow developers to create DB2 Query Views containing response hierarchies?
Item 7 What is the name of the design element in Domino Designer that is a shared resource enabling developers to define DB2 views of data within a DB2-enabled Notes database?	**Item 8** What is the name of the design element in Domino Designer that developers can use to display DB2 data in a view that is populated by an SQL query statement?

Item 2 What does the acronym DAV represent in a Notes database? **DB2 Access View**	**Item 1** What are the special DAV fields that provide metadata about the Notes database containing the DAV? **#AddedToFile, #Created, #Database, #DBPath, #Modified, #OID, #PublicAccess, #Ref, #ReplicaID, #RespInfo, #SequenceNumber, #Server, #UNID**
Item 4 What does the acronym SQL represent? **Structured Query Language**	**Item 3** What does a DB2 Query View use for selection criteria? **SQL query statements**
Item 6 What two special DAV metadata fields allow developers to create DB2 Query Views containing response hierarchies? **#Ref and #RespInfo**	**Item 5** What two special DAV metadata fields allow developers to create functions that can use information related to the location of the Notes database containing the DAV? **#Server and #Database**
Item 8 What is the name of the design element in Domino Designer that developers can use to display DB2 data in a view that is populated by an SQL query statement? **DB2 Query View**	**Item 7** What is the name of the design element in Domino Designer that is a shared resource enabling developers to define DB2 views of data within a DB2-enabled Notes database? **DB2 Access View (DAV)**

Item 9	Item 10
What is displayed at the bottom of the Info tab of the Database Properties to indicate that a Notes database is DB2-enabled?	If an SQL Bulk Update, Delete, or Insert transaction is being processed against a DB2 Access View (DAV) and the operation fails before all rows are processed, what will occur?

Item 11	Item 12
What will happen when saving a new DB2 Access View (DAV) if spaces are entered in the DAV name?	What icon will appear beside the DAV name in the DB2 Access View design list if the DAV was successfully created and populated in DB2?

Item 13	Item 14
If an error occurs during the creation of a new DAV, what icon will appear beside the DAV name in the DB2 Access View design list?	A DB2 Query View can be created to display which of the following? Notes data, federated data, or both?

Item 15	Item 16
What does Lotus Notes and Domino define federated data as?	What is the purpose of the "DB2QueryViewRowLimit" Notes.ini variable?

Item 10

If an SQL Bulk Update, Delete, or Insert transaction is being processed against a DB2 Access View (DAV) and the operation fails before all rows are processed, what will occur?

The entire transaction is rolled back and no rows will be updated, deleted or inserted

Item 9

What is displayed at the bottom of the Info tab of the Database Properties to indicate that a Notes database is DB2-enabled?

The message "Database is DB2 Enabled"

Item 12

What icon will appear beside the DAV name in the DB2 Access View design list if the DAV was successfully created and populated in DB2?

A green check mark

Item 11

What will happen when saving a new DB2 Access View (DAV) if spaces are entered in the DAV name?

The spaces will be converted to underscores

Item 14

A DB2 Query View can be created to display which of the following? Notes data, federated data, or both?

Both

Item 13

If an error occurs during the creation of a new DAV, what icon will appear beside the DAV name in the DB2 Access View design list?

A yellow triangle icon with an exclamation point

Item 16

What is the purpose of the "DB2QueryViewRowLimit" Notes.ini variable?

Limits the maximum number of rows returned in a DB2 Query View from an SQL Query

Item 15

What does Lotus Notes and Domino define federated data as?

Any data that is not stored in a Notes database

Item 17 What is the default for the maximum number of rows returned to a DB2 Query View from an SQL query?	**Item 18** What Notes.ini variable is used to limits the maximum number of rows returned in a DB2 Query View?
Item 19 What will be the impact of including the "DB2QueryViewRowLimit=0" Notes.ini variable in the Notes.ini file of a DB2-enable Domino server?	**Item 20** The "DB2QueryViewRowLimit" Notes.ini variable is stored in the Notes.ini file of which machine? The Domino server or the local machine of the Notes client?
Item 21 What two @Functions can be used to dynamically compose a query for a DB2 Query View?	**Item 22** What two design elements are used in Domino Designer to manage data in DB2-enabled Notes databases?
Item 23 What @Function can be used to dynamically compose a query for a DB2 Query View for Notes client applications?	**Item 24** What @Function can be used to dynamically compose a query for a DB2 Query View for Web applications?

Item 18

What Notes.ini variable is used to limits the maximum number of rows returned in a DB2 Query View?

DB2QueryViewRowLimit=nnn (where nnn is the row limit)

Item 17

What is the default for the maximum number of rows returned to a DB2 Query View from an SQL query?

500 Rows

Item 20

The "DB2QueryViewRowLimit" Notes.ini variable is stored in the Notes.ini file of which machine? The Domino server or the local machine of the Notes client?

Domino server

Item 19

What will be the impact of including the "DB2QueryViewRowLimit=0" Notes.ini variable in the Notes.ini file of a DB2-enable Domino server?

An unlimited number of rows can be returned to a DB2 Query View from an SQL query

Item 22

What two design elements are used in Domino Designer to manage data in DB2-enabled Notes databases?

DB2 Access View and DB2 Query View

Item 21

What two @Functions can be used to dynamically compose a query for a DB2 Query View?

@URLQueryString and @Prompt

Item 24

What @Function can be used to dynamically compose a query for a DB2 Query View for Web applications?

@UrlQueryString

Item 23

What @Function can be used to dynamically compose a query for a DB2 Query View for Notes client applications?

@Prompt

Item 25	Item 26
What is the maximum number of columns that can be included in a DB2 Access View?	The #MODIFIED DAV metadata field returns that same value as what @function?

Item 26

The #MODIFIED DAV metadata field returns that same value as what @function?

@Modified

Item 25

What is the maximum number of columns that can be included in a DB2 Access View?

There is no limit on the number of columns in a DAV

Competency Area 4: Programming Enhancements

Item 1	Item 2
What @Function can be used to determine if the @SetViewInfo function was used to filter documents from a view?	Which LotusScript class is used to handle communications between Composite Application components?

Item 3	Item 4
What method of the NotesDatabase class can be used to create a NotesNoteCollection of all documents in the database that have been read by the current user?	What method of the NotesView class is used to populate a NotesViewEntryCollection with the documents in a view that have been unread by the current user?

Item 5	Item 6
What method of the NotesView class can be used to mark all documents in a view as read by a specified user?	What is the purpose of the Subtract method of the NotesViewEntryCollection class?

Item 7	Item 8
What is the purpose of the Merge method of the NotesViewEntryCollection class?	What @Command can be used to copy selected view entries as a table to the clipboard?

Item 2
Which LotusScript class is used to handle communications between Composite Application components?

NotesPropertyBroker

Item 1
What @Function can be used to determine if the @SetViewInfo function was used to filter documents from a view?

@GetViewInfo([IsViewFiltered])

Item 4
What method of the NotesView class is used to populate a NotesViewEntryCollection with the documents in a view that have been unread by the current user?

GetAllUnreadEntries

Item 3
What method of the NotesDatabase class can be used to create a NotesNoteCollection of all documents in the database that have been read by the current user?

GetAllReadDocuments

Item 6
What is the purpose of the Subtract method of the NotesViewEntryCollection class?

Removes any documents from the NotesViewEntryCollection that exist in the specified secondary collection.

Item 5
What method of the NotesView class can be used to mark all documents in a view as read by a specified user?

MarkAllRead

Item 8
What @Command can be used to copy selected view entries as a table to the clipboard?

@Command([CopySelectedAsTable])

Item 7
What is the purpose of the Merge method of the NotesViewEntryCollection class?

Adds any documents from the NotesViewEntryCollection that exist in the specified secondary collection.

Item 9

In a form design, where are HTML options for the form stored?

Item 10

If both Field-level HTML options and Form-level HTML options exist, which takes precedence?

Item 11

When defining HTML options for the field "Comments", where will these options be stored?

Item 12

In Notes 8, what is the limit of the line length for the LotusScript Write statement?

Item 13

Which LotusScript file handling routines preserve leading spaces in the file name arguments?

Item 14

Which LotusScript file handling routines preserve leading spaces in the file name arguments?

Item 15

What is the name of the @Function that indicates if a view or outline is using the Java user interface?

Item 16

What is the purpose of the GetAllReadDocuments method of the NotesDatabase class?

Item 10 If both Field-level HTML options and Form-level HTML options exist, which takes precedence? **The Field-level HTML options**	**Item 9** In a form design, where are HTML options for the form stored? **$$HTMLOptions text field**
Item 12 In Notes 8, what is the limit of the line length for the LotusScript Write statement? **There is no limit**	**Item 11** When defining HTML options for the field "Comments", where will these options be stored? **$$HTMLOptions_Comments text field**
Item 14 Which LotusScript file handling routines preserve leading spaces in the file name arguments? **Chdir, Filelen, Mkdir, Name, Rmdir**	**Item 13** Which LotusScript file handling routines preserve leading spaces in the file name arguments? **Dir, Filedatetime, Kill, Open, Setfileattr**
Item 16 What is the purpose of the GetAllReadDocuments method of the NotesDatabase class? **Creates a NotesNoteCollection containing all read documents in the database for the current or specified user**	**Item 15** What is the name of the @Function that indicates if a view or outline is using the Java user interface? **@IsUsingJavaElement**

Item 17

What is the feature in Lotus Notes and Domino Release 8 that dynamically compiles Java bytecode to the native platform to optimize performance of Java programs?

Item 18

What will the GetAllUnreadDocuments method of the NotesDatabase class return if the [username] parameter is omitted?

Item 19

What will the GetProfileDocCollection method of the NotesDatabase class return if the [profilename] parameter is omitted?

Item 20

What does the acronym URL represent?

Item 21

What is the maximum amount of data that can be contained in each Request_Content_nnn CGI variable?

Item 22

What field can be configured on a form to disable passthru HTML for the form?

Item 23

What does the acronym RSS represent?

Item 24

What does the acronym JSON represent?

Item 18

What will the GetAllUnreadDocuments method of the NotesDatabase class return if the [username] parameter is omitted?

A NotesNoteCollection containing all unread documents for the current user

Item 17

What is the feature in Lotus Notes and Domino Release 8 that dynamically compiles Java bytecode to the native platform to optimize performance of Java programs?

JIT Compiler

Item 20

What does the acronym URL represent?

Uniform Resource Locator

Item 19

What will the GetProfileDocCollection method of the NotesDatabase class return if the [profilename] parameter is omitted?

A NotesDocumentCollection of all Profile Documents in the database

Item 22

What field can be configured on a form to disable passthru HTML for the form?

$$HTMLOptions

Item 21

What is the maximum amount of data that can be contained in each Request_Content_nnn CGI variable?

64K

Item 24

What does the acronym JSON represent?

JavaScript Object Notation

Item 23

What does the acronym RSS represent?

Really Simple Syndication

Item 25

What does the acronym DXL represent?

Item 26

What does the acronym JIT Compiler represent?

Item 27

Which property of the NotesDXLExporter class can be used to omit rich text pictures and graphics from documents in the DXL output?

Item 28

What is the purpose of the OmitMiscFileObjects property of the NotesDXLExporter class?

Item 29

What is the name of the Domino blog template available in Lotus Notes and Domino Release 8?

Item 30

What is the name of the database template used for creating RSS feeds for views in Notes databases?

Item 31

What @Command can be used to display a calendar view in a two work week display?

Item 32

What @Command can be used to display a calendar view in a one work month display?

Item 26 What does the acronym JIT Compiler represent? **Just-In-Time Compiler**	**Item 25** What does the acronym DXL represent? **Domino XML**
Item 28 What is the purpose of the OmitMiscFileObjects property of the NotesDXLExporter class? **To indicate if miscellaneous file objects are to be excluded from documents in the DXL output**	**Item 27** Which property of the NotesDXLExporter class can be used to omit rich text pictures and graphics from documents in the DXL output? **OmitRichtextPictures property**
Item 30 What is the name of the database template used for creating RSS feeds for views in Notes databases? **RSS_Generator.NTF**	**Item 29** What is the name of the Domino blog template available in Lotus Notes and Domino Release 8? **DominoBlog.NTF**
Item 32 What @Command can be used to display a calendar view in a one work month display? **@Command([CalendarFormat] ; "20")**	**Item 31** What @Command can be used to display a calendar view in a two work week display? **@Command([CalendarFormat] ; "10")**

Item 33 What is the purpose of the @GetViewInfo([IsViewFiltered]) function?	**Item 34** What will the function @Version return for a scheduled agent running on a Domino Release 8.0 Server?
Item 35 The @Command([CalendarFormat] ; "10") formula will display the current calendar view in which format?	**Item 36** The @Command([CalendarFormat] ; "20") formula will display the current calendar view in which format?
Item 37 What is the purpose of the "Outputformat=JSON" argument for the ReadViewEntries URL command?	**Item 38** What type of database can be created from a standard template in Lotus Notes 8 to Map fields in a Notes database to RSS XML elements as well as Generate and Syndicate RSS feeds for a Notes database?
Item 39 What argument should be used with the ReadViewEntries URL command to ensure that the last entry returned is the last entry in a view?	**Item 40** What three data type options can be defined for the KeyType argument of the ReadViewEntries URL command?

Item 34
What will the function @Version return for a scheduled agent running on a Domino Release 8.0 Server?

The string "301" (representing the release number for Notes 8.0)

Item 33
What is the purpose of the @GetViewInfo([IsViewFiltered]) function?

Indicates if the @SetViewInfo function was used to filter documents from a view

Item 36
The @Command([CalendarFormat] ; "20") formula will display the current calendar view in which format?

A one work month display

Item 35
The @Command([CalendarFormat] ; "10") formula will display the current calendar view in which format?

A two work week display

Item 38
What type of database can be created from a standard template in Lotus Notes 8 to Map fields in a Notes database to RSS XML elements as well as Generate and Syndicate RSS feeds for a Notes database?

An RSS feed generator database

Item 37
What is the purpose of the "Outputformat=JSON" argument for the ReadViewEntries URL command?

The view being returned will be displayed in JavaScript Object Notation format

Item 40
What three data type options can be defined for the KeyType argument of the ReadViewEntries URL command?

text, time, number

Item 39
What argument should be used with the ReadViewEntries URL command to ensure that the last entry returned is the last entry in a view?

Endview=1

Item 41

What is the purpose of the "Endview=1" argument for the ReadViewEntries URL command?

Item 42

What argument should be used with the ReadViewEntries URL command to display the view in JavaScript Object Notation format?

Item 43

What argument should be used with the ReadViewEntries URL command to navigate the rows of a view in reverse order?

Item 44

What does the acronym CGI represent?

Item 45

What is the purpose of the AddInternetCertificateToUser method of the NotesAdministrationProcess class in LotusScript?

Item 46

What @Function can be used to determine if a component in a Notes 8 Standard Client is using the Java user interface?

Item 47

Under what circumstances with the CGI variable Request_Content_nnn (where nnn is a sequential number) be used rather than the CGI variable Request_Content?

Item 48

What is the purpose of the @IsUsingJavaElement function?

Item 42

What argument should be used with the ReadViewEntries URL command to display the view in JavaScript Object Notation format?

Outputformat=JSON

Item 41

What is the purpose of the "Endview=1" argument for the ReadViewEntries URL command?

It causes the last entry returned by the URL command to be the last entry in the view

Item 44

What does the acronym CGI represent?

Common Gateway Interface

Item 43

What argument should be used with the ReadViewEntries URL command to navigate the rows of a view in reverse order?

NavigateReverse=1

Item 46

What @Function can be used to determine if a component in a Notes 8 Standard Client is using the Java user interface?

@IsUsingJavaElement

Item 45

What is the purpose of the AddInternetCertificateToUser method of the NotesAdministrationProcess class in LotusScript?

Creates a request in the Administration Requests database to add an Internet certificate for the specified user

Item 48

What is the purpose of the @IsUsingJavaElement function?

It is used to determine if component in a Notes 8 Standard Client is using the Java user interface.

Item 47

Under what circumstances with the CGI variable Request_Content_nnn (where nnn is a sequential number) be used rather than the CGI variable Request_Content?

When an HTTP POST request returns an amount data that exceeds 64K

Item 49 Which LotusScript class is used to perform lookups of a Notes directory?	**Item 50** What is the purpose of the @AbstractSimple function?
Item 51 What is the purpose of the GetAllReadDocuments method of the NotesView class?	**Item 52** What is the purpose of the MarkAllRead method of the NotesView class?
Item 53 Which LotusScript class is used for representing a property in a Composite Application?	**Item 54** A NotesDirectory object in LotusScript can be used to represent a Notes directory on which platform? A Domino server, the local client machine, or both?
Item 55 Which LotusScript class is used to represent a Notes directory?	**Item 56** What is the purpose of the MarkAllUnread method of the NotesViewNavigator class?

Item 50

What is the purpose of the @AbstractSimple function?

Returns a string of either the first 100 characters or first two paragraphs for each text or rich text field specified

Item 49

Which LotusScript class is used to perform lookups of a Notes directory?

NotesDirectoryNavigator

Item 52

What is the purpose of the MarkAllRead method of the NotesView class?

To mark all documents in a view as read by the current or specified user

Item 51

What is the purpose of the GetAllReadDocuments method of the NotesView class?

Populates a NotesViewEntryCollection with the documents in a view that have been read by the current or specified user

Item 54

A NotesDirectory object in LotusScript can be used to represent a Notes directory on which platform? A Domino server, the local client machine, or both?

Both

Item 53

Which LotusScript class is used for representing a property in a Composite Application?

NotesProperty

Item 56

What is the purpose of the MarkAllUnread method of the NotesViewNavigator class?

To mark all documents in a View Navigator as unread by the current or specified user

Item 55

Which LotusScript class is used to represent a Notes directory?

NotesDirectory

Item 57

Which property of the NotesDXLExporter class must be set to True in order to exclude any rich text field attachments from the DXL output?

Item 58

How do you create a new NotesDirectoryNavigator object in LotusScript?

Item 59

Which property of the NotesDirectory class can be set so that only directories containing trust information will be searched by lookups?

Item 60

What is the purpose of the Clone method of the NotesDocumentCollection class?

Item 61

What does it indicate if the Contains method of a NotesDocumentCollection object returns False?

Item 62

What property of the NotesDXLExporter class can be used to specify the format of MIME items in the DXL output?

Item 63

How do you create a new NotesDirectory object in LotusScript?

Item 64

What is the impact to lookup results on a directory when the LimitMatches property of the NotesDirectory object is set to True?

Item 58
How do you create a new NotesDirectoryNavigator object in LotusScript?

By using the CreateNavigator method on a NotesDirectory object

Item 57
Which property of the NotesDXLExporter class must be set to True in order to exclude any rich text field attachments from the DXL output?

OmitRichtextAttachments

Item 60
What is the purpose of the Clone method of the NotesDocumentCollection class?

Creates a new NotesDocumentCollection object that is a copy of the specified NotesDocumentCollection

Item 59
Which property of the NotesDirectory class can be set so that only directories containing trust information will be searched by lookups?

The TrustedOnly property

Item 62
What property of the NotesDXLExporter class can be used to specify the format of MIME items in the DXL output?

MIMEOption

Item 61
What does it indicate if the Contains method of a NotesDocumentCollection object returns False?

One or more of the specified documents are not contained in the NotesDocumentCollection

Item 64
What is the impact to lookup results on a directory when the LimitMatches property of the NotesDirectory object is set to True?

Lookups on that directory will only return the first fifty matches

Item 63
How do you create a new NotesDirectory object in LotusScript?

By using the GetDirectory method of the NotesSession object

Item 65

Which LotusScript class is used for representing an embedded scheduler in the current document?

Item 66

What event is triggered in a NotesUIView object when a user highlights a different row within the current view?

Item 67

Which property of the NotesDirectory class, when set to True, will return matches on partial names for lookups to the directory?

Item 68

Which property of the NotesDXLImporter class, when set to True, will cause the Importer to compile LotusScript code that it encounters?

Item 69

What is the purpose of the Intersect method of the NotesDocumentCollection class?

Item 70

What is the purpose of the GetPropertyBroker method of the NotesSession class?

Item 71

Which property of the NotesUIScheduler class, when set to True, will display checkboxes next to the participants in the embedded scheduler?

Item 72

If the CompileLotusScript property of the NotesDXLImporter object is set to False, when will the LotusScript code that is imported be compiled?

Item 66

What event is triggered in a NotesUIView object when a user highlights a different row within the current view?

The Onselect event

Item 65

Which LotusScript class is used for representing an embedded scheduler in the current document?

NotesUIScheduler

Item 68

Which property of the NotesDXLImporter class, when set to True, will cause the Importer to compile LotusScript code that it encounters?

The CompileLotusScript property

Item 67

Which property of the NotesDirectory class, when set to True, will return matches on partial names for lookups to the directory?

The PartialMatches property

Item 70

What is the purpose of the GetPropertyBroker method of the NotesSession class?

Returns the NotesPropertyBroker object associated with the currently running composite application

Item 69

What is the purpose of the Intersect method of the NotesDocumentCollection class?

Removes any documents from the NotesDocumentCollection that do not also exist in the specified secondary collection.

Item 72

If the CompileLotusScript property of the NotesDXLImporter object is set to False, when will the LotusScript code that is imported be compiled?

When the design note containing the LotusScript code is first used

Item 71

Which property of the NotesUIScheduler class, when set to True, will display checkboxes next to the participants in the embedded scheduler?

DisplayCheckboxes property

Item 73

What is the purpose of the CreateViewNavFromAllRead method of the NotesView class?

Item 74

What method of the NotesUIWorkspace class can be used to reload a specified outline?

Item 75

What is the purpose of the GetAllReadEntries method of the NotesView class?

Item 76

Which property of the NotesDXLExporter class is used to specify which item names are to be included in documents in the DXL output?

Item 77

What method of the NotesView class can be used to create a NotesViewNavigator object containing view entries for the documents in a view that have been unread by the current user?

Item 78

What is the purpose of the OmitItemNames property of the NotesDXLExporter class?

Item 79

The LotusScript "Date" and "Time" statements are not valid on which operating systems?

Item 80

Which property of the NotesDXLExporter class can be used to omit OLE objects from documents in the DXL output?

Item 74 What method of the NotesUIWorkspace class can be used to reload a specified outline? **The OutlineReload method**	**Item 73** What is the purpose of the CreateViewNavFromAllRead method of the NotesView class? **Returns a NotesViewNavigator object containing view entries for the documents in a view that have been read by the current or specified user**
Item 76 Which property of the NotesDXLExporter class is used to specify which item names are to be included in documents in the DXL output? **RestrictToItemNames**	**Item 75** What is the purpose of the GetAllReadEntries method of the NotesView class? **To populate a NotesViewEntryCollection with the documents in a view that have been read by the current or specified user**
Item 78 What is the purpose of the OmitItemNames property of the NotesDXLExporter class? **To specify item names to be excluded from documents in the DXL output**	**Item 77** What method of the NotesView class can be used to create a NotesViewNavigator object containing view entries for the documents in a view that have been unread by the current user? **CreateViewNavFromAllUnread**
Item 80 Which property of the NotesDXLExporter class can be used to omit OLE objects from documents in the DXL output? **OmitOLEObjects property**	**Item 79** The LotusScript "Date" and "Time" statements are not valid on which operating systems? **UNIX and Macintosh OS X**

Item 81 What is the purpose of the RichTextOption property of the NotesDXLExporter class?	**Item 82** Which property of the NotesDXLExporter class can be used to specify whether attachments found in documents should be uncompressed when exported to DXL?
Item 83 How is the JIT compiler activated?	**Item 84** When the WSDL file for a Wiring Property is saved in the Property Broker Editor, what will appear next to the Wiring Property entry in Domino Designer?
Item 85 After a NotesProperty value has been changed using the SetPropertyValue method, what method must be called so that the change is not lost?	**Item 86** What is the default value for the RichTextOption property of the NotesDXLExporter class?
Item 87 What is the default value for the MIMEOption property of the NotesDXLExporter class	**Item 88** Which option is recommended for the MIMEOption property of the NotesDXLExporter class for exporting mail databases?

Item 82

Which property of the NotesDXLExporter class can be used to specify whether attachments found in documents should be uncompressed when exported to DXL?

UncompressAttachments

Item 81

What is the purpose of the RichTextOption property of the NotesDXLExporter class?

To indicate the format to use for rich text items found in documents when exporting to DXL.

Item 84

When the WSDL file for a Wiring Property is saved in the Property Broker Editor, what will appear next to the Wiring Property entry in Domino Designer?

A circled arrow

Item 83

How is the JIT compiler activated?

It is activated by default

Item 86

What is the default value for the RichTextOption property of the NotesDXLExporter class?

RICHTEXTOPTION_DXL (0)

Item 85

After a NotesProperty value has been changed using the SetPropertyValue method, what method must be called so that the change is not lost?

The Publish method

Item 88

Which option is recommended for the MIMEOption property of the NotesDXLExporter class for exporting mail databases?

MIMEOPTION_DXL (0)

Item 87

What is the default value for the MIMEOption property of the NotesDXLExporter class?

MIMEOPTION_RAW (1)

Competency Area 5: Web Services in Domino Applications

Item 1

What types of Web Services does Domino Designer 8 support? Consumer Web Services, Provider Web Services, or both?

Item 2

A consumer web service in a Domino database can be coded in which programming language(s)?

Item 3

How is a web service consumer created in Domino Designer?

Item 4

What three sub-actions are available in the "WSDL" action button in a LotusScript Library?

Item 5

What does Domino Designer do to the WSDL code when a WSDL file is imported into a LotusScript script library via the "WSDL > Import WSDL" button?

Item 6

What does the acronym WSDL represent?

Item 7

What does the acronym XML represent?

Item 8

How do you initiate a local preview of a Web Service?

Item 2
A consumer web service in a Domino database can be coded in which programming language(s)?

LotusScript or Java

Item 1
What types of Web Services does Domino Designer 8 support? Consumer Web Services, Provider Web Services, or both?

Both

Item 4
What three sub-actions are available in the "WSDL" action button in a LotusScript Library?

Show WSDL, Import WSDL, Export WSDL

Item 3
How is a web service consumer created in Domino Designer?

By creating a web service enabled script library and importing the WSDL associated with the web service

Item 6
What does the acronym WSDL represent?

Web Services Description Language

Item 5
What does Domino Designer do to the WSDL code when a WSDL file is imported into a LotusScript script library via the "WSDL > Import WSDL" button?

Converts the WSDL code to LotusScript

Item 8
How do you initiate a local preview of a Web Service?

Open the Web Service design element and select "Design > Preview in Default Web Browser" from the menu

Item 7
What does the acronym XML represent?

eXtensible Markup Language

Item 9

What does Domino Designer do to the WSDL code when a WSDL file is imported into a Java script library via the "WSDL > Import WSDL" button?

Item 10

After a script library has been web service enabled, how can it be un-enabled?

Item 11

What does the acronym SOAP represent?

Item 12

What menu choice in the client can be used to stop the Web browser preview of a Web Service without exiting Notes?

Item 13

What will happen if you re-import a WSDL file into a Web Service enabled script library after it has been customized?

Item 14

What is the name of the text file that is created in the Notes data directory when a WSDL file in imported into a LotusScript script library?

Item 15

When importing a WSDL file into a LotusScript script library, where will the text file "WSNamespace.mappings" be stored?

Item 16

Which type of Web Service requires the use of a script library in Domino Designer? Consumer Web Service, Provider Web Service, or both?

Item 10

After a script library has been web service enabled, how can it be un-enabled?

It can't. Once a script library has been web service enabled, it cannot be un-enabled.

Item 9

What does Domino Designer do to the WSDL code when a WSDL file is imported into a Java script library via the "WSDL > Import WSDL" button?

Converts the WSDL code to Java

Item 12

What menu choice in the client can be used to stop the Web browser preview of a Web Service without exiting Notes?

File > Tools > Stop Local Web Preview Process

Item 11

What does the acronym SOAP represent?

Simple Object Access Protocol

Item 14

What is the name of the text file that is created in the Notes data directory when a WSDL file in imported into a LotusScript script library?

WSNamespace.mappings

Item 13

What will happen if you re-import a WSDL file into a Web Service enabled script library after it has been customized?

Any customizations to the script library will be overwritten

Item 16

Which type of Web Service requires the use of a script library in Domino Designer? Consumer Web Service, Provider Web Service, or both?

Consumer Web Service

Item 15

When importing a WSDL file into a LotusScript script library, where will the text file "WSNamespace.mappings" be stored?

In the Notes data directory

Item 17

Which type of Web Service requires the use of a script library in Domino Designer? Consumer Web Service, Provider Web Service, or both?

Item 18

What statement must be included in the Declarations section of an agent in order to invoke a consumer Web Service from that agent?

Item 18

What statement must be included in the Declarations section of an agent in order to invoke a consumer Web Service from that agent?

A "Use" statement with the name of the script library containing the consumer Web Service

Item 17

Which type of Web Service requires the use of a script library in Domino Designer? Consumer Web Service, Provider Web Service, or both?

Consumer Web Service

Chapter 7

Study Notes

Acronyms

ACL - Access Control List
Blog - Web Log
CAE - Composite Application Editor
CGI - Common Gateway Interface
DAV - DB2 Access View
DXL - Domino XML
G (GB) - Gigabyte (1,024 Megabytes or 1,073,741,824 Bytes)
HTML - Hypertext Markup Language
HTTP - Hypertext Transfer Protocol
JSON - JavaScript Object Notation)
K (KB) - Kilobyte (1,024 Bytes)
M (MB) - Megabyte (1,024 Kilobytes or 1,048,576 Bytes)
MIME - Multipurpose Internet Mail Extensions
NSF - Notes Storage Facility
ODS - On-Disk Structure
PBE - Property Broker Editor
RSS - Really Simple Syndication
SOA - Service Oriented Architecture
SOAP - Simple Object Access Protocol
SQL - Structured Query Language
T (TB) - Terabyte (1,024 Terabytes or 1,099,511,627,776 Bytes)
URL - Uniform Resource Locator
WSDL - Web Services Description Language
XML - Extensible Markup Language

New Client Architecture

Lotus Notes 8 Standard Client
- Eclipsed-based User Interface (UI)
- Supports Composite Applications

Lotus Notes 8 Basic Client
- Same architecture as earlier Notes Client releases

New Design Element Features

Actions:
- Disable the Action Bar Properties setting "Show default items in right-mouse menu" to hide default system actions in a view or folder right-click context menu
- Split Button Action
  - Click on the main part of the button (left side) to execute first sub-action
  - Click on down arrow on right side of button to display all sub-actions
  - Only available for views and folders
  - Only available for composite applications

Agents:
- New Event Trigger - When Server Starts

Column Settings:
- New Number Format - Bytes(K/M/G)
  - Displays suffix of K (Kilobytes), M (Megabytes), G (Gigabytes), or T (Terabytes)
  - The suffix displayed is dependent on the size of number value in column
  - Kilobyte (K) = 1024 Bytes
  - Megabyte (M) = 1,048,576 Bytes (1024 Kilobytes)
  - Gigabyte (G) = 1,073,741,824 Bytes (1024 Megabytes)
  - Terabyte (T) = 1,099,511,627,776 Bytes (1024 Gigabytes)
  - Numbers are rounded, but never less than 1K
  - Kilobytes display whole numbers only
  - One decimal place is displayed for Megabytes, Gigabytes, and Terabytes
- The setting "Extend to use available window width" allows any column to be extended to use the available window width of a view or folder
- The setting "Defer index creation until first use" defers creation of the sort index for a user-sorted column until a user clicks on the column header to re-sort the view

View features for Eclipsed-based User Interface (UI):
- Hide Column Header – Shows column data only, without a column heading
- Partial Response Hierarchies - Missing roots of partial threads are created to show hierarchical response trees
- Vertical/Horizontal Switcher – displays icons in the action bar of the view to allow user to switch between horizontal and vertical layouts
- Tab Navigator – Displays button icons to control sets of documents displayed in viewer
- Thread View – Allows user to switch between message mode and the conversation mode
- Viewers – Users can switch between the following types of viewers:
  - Table
    - Also known as Narrow View or Vertical View
    - Options: Keep on top, Hide this column, Wrap to second row
    - Up to two rows can be displayed per entry
    - The setting "Justify second row under this column" indents second row
  - Calendar
  - Tiled
    - Also known as a Business Card layout
    - Options: Display on top, Display on bottom, Hide this column
    - Vertical scrolling only
  - Third Party Viewers

Forms:
- New option to display checkboxes next to the participants in an embedded scheduler
- HTML Options for a form
  - Used for controlling the HTML generated for the entire form
  - HTML Options can be defined at form or field level
  - Form level HTML Options will be overridden by field level HTML Options
  - HTML options are specified by name=value pairs
  - Multiple HTML Options may be specified if the field is configured to allow multiple values
  - Form level HTML Options are stored in a special field - $$HTMLOption:
    - The DisablePassThruHTML option disables passthru HTML on the form, causing the HTML to be treated as plain text.
    - The ForceSectionExpand option will force all sections on the form to be expanded.
    - The ForceOutlineExpand option will force all outlines on the form to be expanded.
    - The RowAtATimeTableAlt option will force all rows of a tabbed table to be displayed on the form.
    - The TextExactSpacing option will preserve multiple spaces between characters when displayed on the form.

Fields:
- Thumbnail option in Rich Text Lite field:
  - Displays a fixed size image when "Resize Thumbnail Image, in pixels" setting is used
  - When Thumbnail option is selected, an image attachment name must be specified
  - When Thumbnail option is selected, all other options are automatically deselected
  - When an option other than Thumbnail is selected, the Thumbnail option is automatically deselected
- HTML Options for a specific field
  - Used for controlling the HTML generated for the field
  - HTML Options can be defined at field or form level
  - Field level HTML Options will override form level HTML Options
  - Field level HTML Options are stored in a special field - $$HTMLOption_fieldname
  - DisablePassThruHTML options:
    - Use "DisablePassThruHTML=0" to allow all passthru HTML for the field
    - Use "DisablePassThruHTML=1" to disable passthru HTML delimited with HTML tags [< and >]
    - Use "DisablePassThruHTML=2" to disable passthru HTML with the Notes editor "Pass-Thru HTML" paragraph style
    - Use "DisablePassThruHTML=4" to disable passthru HTML marked with the rich text passthru attribute
    - Use "DisablePassThruHTML=7" to disable all passthru HTML (i.e. delimited with HTML tags [< and >], indicated with the Notes editor "Pass-Thru HTML" paragraph style, and marked with the rich text passthru attribute)

Outlines:
- Horizontal separators between outline entries can be displayed for users running the Lotus Notes 8 Standard Client

New Database Performance Features

Database Properties setting "Don't allow simple search":
- In Advanced Tab of Database Properties
- Prevents searches against a database that is not full-text indexed
- Displays error message "Application must be full text indexed before search is allowed"

Database Properties setting "Support Response Thread History":
- In Advanced Tab of Database Properties
- Adds the field $TUA to new documents. This field contains additional information for sorting documents into a document response hierarchy.
- Impacts new documents only. Existing documents are not updated with the additional information fields.

Column Properties setting "Defer index creation until first use":
- Defers creation of sort indices for user-sorted columns until users re-sort the columns
- Requires the Notes.ini variable "ENABLE_ON_DEMAND_COLLATIONS=1" to be included in the Notes.ini file of the Domino server.

New Java Support Features

New Java 5 Support in Lotus Notes Domino Release 8:
- Supports Java 5 Syntax
- Garbage Collection process improvements
- Just-In-Time (JIT) compiler
  - Dynamically compiles Java bytecode to the native platform to optimize performance of Java programs
  - The JIT compiler is activated by default

New Web Application Features

Optional arguments for ReadViewEntries URL Command:
- EndView=1
  - Ensures that the last entry returned is the last entry in the view.
  - Combine with the "Count=n" argument to return the last "n" entries of the view
- NavigateReverse=1
  - Navigates the rows of a view in reverse order
- Outputformat=JSON
  - Displays a view in the JavaScript Object Notation format
- Keytype=number
  - Specifies the data type for the StartKey argument as a number (prior to Release 8, the only options for the KeyType value were text or time)

CGI variable Request_Content_nnn:
- Used in place of the Request_Content CGI variable when an HTTP POST request returns more than 64K of data
- Request_Content_000 will contain the first 64K of data, Request_Content_001 will contain the next 64K of data, and so on.

New Formula Language Features

@Functions:
- @GetViewInfo([IsViewFiltered])
  - Indicates if @SetViewInfo was used to filter documents from a view
  - Useful for view action hide/when formulas
- @URLQueryString
  - Can be used to dynamically compose a query for a DB2 Query View
- @AbstractSimple
  - Returns first 100 characters or first two paragraphs of text or rich text fields
- @Version
  - Returns the string "301" to represent the release number for Notes 8.0
- @IsUsingJavaElement
  - Indicates if a view or outline in the Standard Notes 8 Client is using the Java user interface

@Commands
- @Command([CopySelectedAsTable])
  - Copies the selected entries of a view, including DocLinks, to the clipboard as a table
  - Selected entries may be documents, categories, calendar entries, or totals
- @Command([OpenInNewWindow])
  - Opens selected document in a new window in the Notes client
- @Command([CalendarFormat])
  - Two new calendar format options for Release 8: Options "10" and "20"
  - Calendar format option "10" specifies a two work week display
  - Calendar format option "20" specifies a one work month display

New LotusScript Language Features

Classes:
- NotesDirectory class - New class
  - Represents the directories on a specified server
  - Associated with one or more directory navigators
  - Created with the GetDirectory method of the NotesSession class
- NotesDirectoryNavigator class - New class
  - Used for performing lookups of a Notes directory
  - Created with the CreateNavigator method of the NotesDirectory class
- NotesProperty class - New class
  - Represents a composite application property
- NotesPropertyBroker class - New class
  - Used for communication between components of a composite application
  - Created with the GetPropertyBroker method of the NotesSession class

Events:
- OnSelect event of the NotesUIView class - New event
  - Triggered when view is opened
  - Triggered when a document is selected in the "selection margin"
  - Triggered when a document is deselected in the "selection margin"
  - Triggered when a user selects a document that is already selected

Properties:
- New properties in the NotesUIScheduler class
  - DisplayCheckboxes property
    - Indicates if checkboxes are displayed next to participants in embedded scheduler
- New properties in the NotesDXLImporter class
  - CompileLotusScript property
    - True (the default) indicates that the DXL Importer will compile LotusScript code as it is imported
    - False indicate that the design note containing the LotusScript code will be compiled when first used
- New properties in the NotesDXLExporter class
  - MIMEOption property
    - Specifies format of MIME items in the DXL output
    - MIMEOPTION_DXL (0) indicates that MIME items are exported in DXL as a <mime> element. Recommended when exporting mail databases.
    - MIMEOPTION_RAW (1) indicates that each MIME item is exported as an <item> with a <rawitemdata> element containing the raw data for the MIME item. The raw data is encoded in Base64. This is the default for this option and was the only DXL format for MIME items prior to Release 8.
  - RichTextOption property
    - Specifies format of rich text items in the DXL output
    - RICHTEXTOPTION_DXL (0) indicates that rich text items are exported in DXL format as a <richtext> element. This is the default for this option.
    - RICHTEXTOPTION_RAW (1) indicates that rich text items are exported as a <rawitemdata> element containing the raw data for the rich text item. The raw data is encoded in Base64. Useful when database being exported is to be imported into another database, because the imported data will be identical to the original data.
  - OmitItemNames property
    - Lists item names that are to be omitted from documents in the DXL output.
    - The OmitItemNames property overrides the RestrictToItemNames property.
    - If the exported DXL will be imported at a later time by the DXL Importer, the imported documents will not include the items that were omitted by this option.
  - RestrictToItemNames property
    - Lists only those items from documents that will be included in the DXL output.
    - The OmitItemNames property overrides the RestrictToItemNames property.
    - If the exported DXL will be imported at a later time by the DXL Importer, the imported documents will not include items that were excluded by this option.
  - OmitMiscFileObject property
    - Indicates if miscellaneous file objects within documents should be excluded from DXL output.
    - Miscellaneous file objects are non-standard attachments (not related to $File items), that are stored as file objects. These file attachment items are often application-specific data.
  - OmitOLEObjects property
    - Indicates if OLE objects ($File items) within documents should be excluded from DXL output.
  - OLEObjectOmittedText property
    - Indicates the text to be inserted within exported rich text items where an <objectref> element was omitted via the OmitOLEObjects property.

Properties (continued):
- New properties in the NotesDXLExporter class (continued):
  - OmitRichtextAttachments property
    - Indicates if attachments ($File items) within documents should be excluded from DXL output.
  - AttachmentOmittedText property
    - Indicates the text to be inserted within exported rich text items where an <attachmentref> element was omitted via the OmitRichtextAttachments property.
  - OmitRichtextPictures property
    - Indicates if rich text pictures/graphics within documents should be excluded from DXL output.
    - Omits <picture> elements within document rich text items that contain <gif>, <jpeg>, <notesbitmap>, or <cgm> elements.
    - Pictures/graphics within <imagemap> elements will not be omitted.
    - Pictures/graphics within <attachmentref> elements will not be omitted unless attachments are also omitted (using the OmitRichtextAttachments property).
  - PictureOmittedText property
    - Indicates the text to be inserted within exported rich text items where a <picture> element was omitted via the OmitRichtextAttachments property.
  - UncompressAttachments property
    - Indicates if document attachments should be compressed in the DXL output.
    - If the exported DXL will be imported at a later time by the DXL Importer, these attachments will be recompressed unless the desiredcompression attribute is removed from the DXL programmatically.

Methods:
- New methods in the NotesSession class
  - GetDirectory method
    - Returns a NotesDirectory object for the specified server
  - GetPropertyBroker method
    - Returns a NotesPropertyBroker object for the property broker that is associated with the current composite application
- New methods in the NotesDatabase class
  - GetAllReadDocuments method
    - Creates a NotesNoteCollection of all read documents in the database for the current or specified user (includes both data and design notes)
    - If the username option is omitted, returns documents for the current user
  - GetAllUnreadDocuments method
    - Creates a NotesNoteCollection of all unread documents in the database for the current or specified user (includes both data and design notes)
    - If the username option is omitted, returns documents for the current user
  - GetProfileDocCollection method
    - If the profilename option is omitted (optional beginning with Release 8), all profile documents in the database are returned in the document collection.
- New methods in the NotesDocument class
  - MarkRead method
    - Marks a document as read by the current or specified user
    - If the username option is omitted, marks the document for the current user
  - MarkUnread method
    - Marks a document as unread by the current or specified user
    - If the username option is omitted, marks the document for the current user

Methods (continued):
- New methods in the NotesDocumentCollection class:
  - Clone method
    - Returns a new NotesDocumentCollection object which is a copy of the current NotesDocumentCollection object
  - Contains method
    - Indicates if the NotesDocumentCollection object contains a specified document or all documents in a specified collection
  - Intersect method
    - Removes any documents from the NotesDocumentCollection object that are not also contained in the specified collection
  - Merge method
    - Adds documents to the NotesDocumentCollection object that are not already in the collection but are contained in the specified collection
  - Subtract method
    - Removes any documents from the NotesDocumentCollection object that are contained in the specified collection
  - MarkAllRead method
    - Marks all documents in the NotesDocumentCollection as read by the current or specified user
    - If the username option is omitted, marks the documents for the current user
  - MarkAllUnread method
    - Marks all documents in the NotesDocumentCollection as unread by the current or specified user
    - If the username option is omitted, marks the documents for the current user
- New methods in the NotesViewEntryCollection class
  - Clone method
    - Returns a new NotesViewEntryCollection object which is a copy of the current NotesViewEntryCollection object
  - Contains method
    - Indicates if the NotesViewEntryCollection object contains an entry that represents a specified document or all entries that represent the documents in a specified collection
  - Intersect method
    - Removes any entries from the NotesViewEntryCollection object that represent documents that are not also contained in the specified collection
  - Merge method
    - Adds entries to the NotesViewEntryCollection object that are not already in the collection but represent documents that are contained in the specified collection
  - Subtract method
    - Removes any entries from the NotesViewEntryCollection object that represent documents that are contained in the specified collection
  - MarkAllRead method
    - Marks all documents represented by entries in the NotesViewEntryCollection as read by the current or specified user
    - If the username option is omitted, marks the documents for the current user
  - MarkAllUnread method
    - Marks all documents represented by entries in the NotesViewEntryCollection as unread by the current or specified user
    - If the username option is omitted, marks the documents for the current user

Methods (continued):
- New methods in the NotesViewNavigator class
  - MarkAllRead method
    - Marks all documents represented by entries in the NotesViewNavigator as read by the current or specified user
    - If the username option is omitted, marks the documents for the current user
  - MarkAllUnread method
    - Marks all documents represented by entries in the NotesViewNavigator as unread by the current or specified user
    - If the username option is omitted, marks the documents for the current user
- New methods in the NotesUIWorkspace class
  - OutlineReload method
    - Reloads the specified outline for the specified database

Statements:
- Write statement - There is no limit on the line length of a line written by the Write statement (there was a limit of 255 characters in Release 7)

New Design Templates

RSS Feed Generator:
- Design template name for creating an RSS Feed Generator databases is "RSS_Generator.ntf"
- Contains agents and script libraries for generating RSS feeds for views in Notes databases
- An RSS Feed Definition form is completed for each RSS feed defined in the RSS Feed Generator database
- RSS Feed Generator databases must reside on a Domino server
- An RSS Feed Generator database can only access databases residing on the same Domino server
- Primary functions of an RSS Feed Generator database:
  - Map fields from Notes databases to RSS XML elements
  - Generate RSS feeds for views in Notes databases
  - Syndicate/advertise the RSS feeds that have been generated
- When an RSS Feed Generator database is opened, users are redirected to the "Available Feeds" page

Domino Blog (Web Log)
- Design template name for creating a Domino Blog database is "DominoBlog.ntf"
- Domino Blog databases can be accessed and maintained from either a Notes client or a Web browser
- Includes the following HTML templates to control the "look and feel" of the blog:
  - Page Templates - Controls appearance of Web page layout
  - Item Templates - Controls appearance of the content lists
  - Block Templates - Simplifies HTML template maintenance
  - Web Client Template - Controls appearance of the Web editor

New Web Services Features

Consumer Web Services:
- In addition to Provider Web Services, Consumer Web Services can now be created in Domino Designer in Release 8
- A Consumer Web Service is created by creating a Web Service enabled script library
- A Provider Web Service is created with the Web Service design element
- Web Services can be created in either LotusScript or Java
- The WSDL for a consumer Web Service is imported into a Web Service enabled script library
- The "WSDL" action button in a script library contains three sub-actions:
  - Show WSDL
  - Import WSDL
  - Export WSDL
- Importing a WSDL file into a Web Service enabled LotusScript script library converts the WSDL to LotusScript code
- Importing a WSDL file into a Web Service enabled Java script library converts the WSDL to Java code
- Once a script library has been Web Service enabled, it cannot be un-enabled as a Web Service
- Re-importing a WSDL file into an existing Web Service enabled script library will overwrite any customizations

Preview Web Services locally:
- Previewing a Web Service is similar to previewing other design elements:
  - Select "Design > Preview in Default Web Browser" from the menu
  - Displays a form in the browser with a link to the Web Service's WSDL document
- To stop the Web browser preview without exiting Notes, select "File > Tools > Stop Local Web Preview Process"

Combining script libraries for greater efficiency:
- Namespaces allow elements and attributes of WSDL files to be treated as unique names
- Importing a WSDL file into a LotusScript script library will create the text file "WSNamespace.mappings":
  - Records WSDL namespaces and associated LotusScript constants
  - WSNamespace.mappings file is maintained in user's Notes Data directory

New DB2 Integration Features

New DB2 Access View (DAV) metadata fields:
- #ADDEDTOFILE, #CREATED, #DATABASE, #DBPATH, #MODIFIED, #OID, #PUBLICACCESS, #REF, #REPLICAID, #RESPINFO, #SEQUENCENUMBER, #SERVER, #UNID
- #SERVER and #DATABASE contains information related to the location of the Notes database containing the DAV
- #REF and #RESPINFO contains information for developers to create DB2 Query Views containing response hierarchies
- #UNID is now a 32 bit string (was a 16 bit binary value in Release 7)
- #MODIFIED now returns that same value as the @Modified function (the #MODIFIED metadata field was not synonymous with the @Modified function in Release 7)

DB2 Access View (DAV):
- A shared resource design element enabling developers to define DB2 views of data within a DB2-enabled Notes database
- There is no limit on the number of columns in a DB2 Access View
- A yellow database/view icon with starburst indicates a new DAV not yet created or populated in DB2
- A gray database/view icon indicates a new DAV was been created in DB2, but not yet populated
- A green check mark beside DAV in design list indicates DAV was successfully created and populated in DB2
- A yellow triangle icon with an exclamation point indicates an error occurred during the creation of a new DAV

DB2 Query View:
- A design element that developers can use to display DB2 data in a view
- Uses SQL to populate view entries
- Displays Notes data, federated data, or a combination of Notes and federated data
- DB2 Query views are dynamic and are recalculated when view is opened or refreshed
- The Notes.ini variable "DB2QueryViewRowLimit" limits the number of rows returned in a DB2 Query View from an SQL Query

New Composite Application Features

Composite Application - Architecture and Planning
- Uses Service Oriented Architecture (SOA)
  - Reusable components
  - Loosely coupled services
- Composite Application Components
  - NSF (Notes) Components
  - Eclipse Components
  - Composite Applications can consist of multiple components from multiple sources
  - Components are "wired together" to interact with each other via the property broker feature
- Composite Applications on the Notes Client
  - Supported only on the Lotus Note 8 Standard Client
    - Built on the Lotus Expeditor framework, which is built on the Eclipse framework

Creating Composite Applications
- Create a Composite Application Container
  - Several methods can be used to create a Composite Application Container for running on the Lotus Notes 8 Standard client:
    - Create a new Notes application using the "Blank Composite Application" template
    - Select the "New Blank CA" button from the "Composite Applications > Applications" view in Domino Designer 8
    - Select the "Import XML" button from the "Composite Applications > Applications" view in Domino Designer 8 to import an existing Composite Application XML file into an existing Notes application
  - In the Launch tab of the Application Properties, select "Launch as Composite Application"

Creating Composite Applications (continued)
- Design and build the components
  - NSF Components are built using Domino Designer 8
  - Eclipse Components are built using an Eclipse integrated development environment (IDE), Rational Application Developer, or Lotus Expeditor
  - The Property Broker Editor (PBE) generates WSDL files for component interaction
    - Launched from the Domino Designer 8 client
- Assemble and wire the components
  - Use the Composite Application Editor to assemble and wire Composite Application components
    - Launched from Lotus Notes 8 Standard client

Deploying Composite Applications
- Composite Applications may be hosted in the following environments:
  - Domino 8 server
  - WebSphere Portal server
  - Local machine of a Lotus Notes 8 Standard client
- A Composite Applications hosted on a Domino 8 server can only be accessed from a Lotus Notes 8 Standard client, and not from a Web browser
- A Composite Applications hosted on a WebSphere Portal server can be accessed from a Web browser as well as a Lotus Notes 8 Standard client

Property Broker Editor (PBE)
- Launched from the Domino Designer 8 client
  - Select a WSDL file in the "Composite Applications > Wiring Properties" view and click the "Open File" action button
- Used for creating and editing the WSDL files for the Composite Application Properties design elements
  - The WSDL files are used to define the following for the property broker feature:
    - Properties
    - Actions
    - Types (for data items)

Composite Application Editor (CAE)
- Launched from the Lotus Notes 8 Standard client
  - Open a composite application in the Lotus Notes 8 client and select "Actions > Edit Application"
- Used for assembling and editing composite applications
  - Add new composite application components
  - Edit composite application components
  - Wire composite application components together
- When changes are saved in the Composite Application Editor those changes will be reflected immediately in the composite application running on the Lotus Notes client
  - Modify the application
    - Add pages
    - Edit roles and application properties
  - Modify the application pages
    - Add, delete, and rename pages
    - Edit page properties
  - Modify the application components
    - Add and delete components,
    - Edit wires and component properties

Composite Application Design Elements
- Wiring Properties Design Element
  - Represented as WSDL files
    - Define data types, properties, and actions
  - Create a new Wiring Properties design element:
    - From the "Composite Applications > Wiring Properties" view, select the "New Wiring Properties" button
    - Enter a name for the new design element, select the OK button, and a new blank Wiring Properties design element is created
    - Select the "Open File" button, which launches the Property Broker Editor, so that the properties, actions, and data types can be defined
  - Import an existing WSDL file into the Composite Application Container:
    - From the "Composite Applications > Wiring Properties" view, select the "Import WSDL" button to import a WSDL from the file system
  - Update a WSDL file in the Composite Application Container:
    - From the "Composite Applications > Wiring Properties" view, select the "Export WSDL" button to export a WSDL to the file system
    - Edit and save the WSDL file
    - Use the Refresh button to re-import the WSDL file into the Composite Application Container
  - Merge multiple WSDL files into a single WSDL file:
    - From the "Composite Applications-Wiring Properties" view, select the WSDL files to merge and select the "Merge WSDLs" button
    - In the "Save As" dialog box, specify the directory and filename for the merged WSDL file and select the OK button
  - View and/or edit WSDL file contents using one of these methods:
    - From the "Composite Applications > Wiring Properties" view, select the WSDL file and select the "Open File" button
      - The Property Broker Editor will be launched with the selected WSDL file
    - From the "Composite Applications > Wiring Properties" view, select the WSDL file and select the "Open With" button
      - You must then select the application that will be used to view and/or edit the WSDL file (e.g. Notepad or some other text editor)
- Applications Design Element
  - Represented as XML files
    - Defines the composite application
    - Stored in the composite application container of a composite application
  - Import an existing composite application XML file:
    - From the "Composite Applications > Applications" view, select the "Import XML" button to import a XML file from the file system
  - Update an existing composite application XML file:
    - From the "Composite Applications > Applications" view, select the "Export XML" button to store the XML file on the local file system
    - Edit the exported XML file
    - Re-import the updated XML file by selecting the Refresh button
  - Create a new composite application XML file:
    - From the "Composite Applications > Application" view, select the "New Comp App" button
    - Enter a name for the new composite application, select the OK button, and a new composite application XML design element is created

Chapter 8

Certification Testing Tips

About the Certification Exam

Following is some information that you'll need to know about Certification Exam 801:

Exam Number:	190-801
Exam Name:	IBM Lotus Notes Domino 8 Application Development Update
Exam Format:	Multiple Choice
Duration of Exam:	105 Minutes
Passing Score:	75%
Total Questions:	60

As you take the exam, you may skip questions and/or mark questions for later review. During the course of the exam, you may return to any of the previous questions. Prior to completing the exam, you will be given an opportunity to review a list of the question numbers and determine which have been completed, skipped, and/or marked for review. You may then return to any of the questions that you feel require additional attention.

After you mark your exam as complete, the exam will automatically be graded. Your score, as well as a message indicating if you passed of failed the exam, will be displayed. An Examination Score Report will also be printed. This report will display your score, the minimum passing score, and a grade of either "Pass" or "Fail". The report also displays a breakdown of how you scored in each of the exam competency areas.

From the Author

I've been taking certification exams for most of my IT career. Certifications serve as an industry benchmark, demonstrating to current and/or prospective employers and clients that you have acquired the knowledge and skills necessary to perform at the specified level of certification. As a consultant and instructor, I find it absolutely necessary to keep my certifications up-to-date.

I've taken over 20 certification exams for just the Lotus Certification Program alone. I tend to "over-prepare" for my exams (just ask my family, friends, and colleagues), spending many hours researching, taking notes, testing, etc. for each exam. However, I've never been disappointed in my results. In fact, I've never failed a Lotus certification exam, and I typically score over 90%.

Over the years, I have developed a proven method for certification exam preparation (at least it's worked for me!). Here is an example of the steps I use in preparing for an exam:

- Gather and research all of the material related to the exam that I can get my hands on (product documentation, IBM Redbooks, developerWorks articles and tutorials, Help databases, release notes, etc.).
- Create test servers and "stuff tester" databases in order to try out exam related features, configurations, etc.
- Look for opportunities to incorporate exam related features into my environment so that I can become familiar with them.
- Organize the results of my research into flash cards and study notes.

While you can take advantage of the many hours that I've devoted to preparing the study material for this certification exam, I strongly encourage you to try out all of the exam related features yourself before taking the actual exam. Build yourself a test environment and "play around" a bit.

Exam Taking Tips

The Lotus Notes certification program describes their certification exams as "performance-based" exams. This means that many of the questions in the exam require that you solve a business problem presented in a scenario. While the answers to these types of questions are multiple choice, you must be careful to fully understand the business problem being presented in the scenario before choosing the correct answer.

Whether the question and possible answers appear to be simple and straight forward, or complicated and scenario-based, be wary of certain key words that might be overlooked if you rush through the exam. Don't fall into the trap of just looking at the possible answers and choosing one that looks reasonable. The question associated with that answer might very well contain the word "not" or "false", which would make that answer completely wrong. Before choosing your answer for a question, first eliminate all of the answers that you are certain are incorrect. Some questions may appear to have more than one correct answer. You must choose the one that best answers the question.

And finally, don't over-analyze the questions and answers. Remember, these exams are developed with the "ideal world" in mind, and not the "real world" that we live and work in. If a feature described in a question doesn't behave quite the way that it does in your environment, make sure that you are answering the question related to how that feature is described in the product documentation.

A good strategy to use is to take at least two passes over the exam. During the first pass, answer those questions that you a completely confident about and consider yourself done with those questions (your first instinct in these cases is usually correct). Also during the first pass, when you encounter a question that you are not completely confident about, mark it to be reviewed during then next pass. If you encounter a question for which you have absolutely no clue about how to answer it, it might be a good idea to skip that question during the first pass. It's possible that subsequent questions will provide key information to help you answer it. During the second pass, go to those questions that you marked for review or skipped during the first pass. As you confirm or alter your original answer, unmark that question. If you're still not certain about your answer, leave the question marked. You may have time for a third pass. Before you mark the exam as complete, review the list of question numbers for any items that were skipped. It's better to take a guess at an answer than to leave a question incomplete. You have a 25% chance of getting the correct answer if you guess, but a 0% chance of getting the correct answer if you leave the question incomplete.

Good luck on your exam!

www.ingramcontent.com/pod-product-compliance
Lightning Source LLC
Chambersburg PA
CBHW051213200326
41519CB00025B/7101